# THUMBS UP!

*Best Wishes*

*Fred Perkins*

# SIR FRED PONTIN

## MY HAPPY LIFE. ALWAYS...
## Thumbs Up!

SOLO *books*

Published by Solo Books Ltd.,
49–53 Kensington High Street,
London W8 5ED, England

First Published 1991

Copyright © Sir Fred Pontin and Peter Willsher, 1991

ISBN 1 873939 00 0

Set in 10/12 Sabon.

Printed in Great Britain by G.P. Printers,
South Molton, Devon.

# ACKNOWLEDGEMENTS

WHEN Peter Willsher mentioned that it was high time the story of my life was published and that he was willing to devote his considerable energies in gathering together all of the necessary information to this end, I decided that he had a point.

Many of my friends had been urging me to set down on paper just how it was that I came to create such a successful holiday business after my pre-war career in the City of London and also to let people know how I got so involved with charitable activities and horse racing.

Peter has been known to me for many years and there have been times when I wish that I had reacted more positively to investing in some of his own ventures, especially his new marina at Shotley Point and previously a property development opportunity near Tower Bridge. In these circumstances it would have been churlish not to react favourably to his encouraging remarks about writing this book.

Now that the work has been completed I must confess to being very happy that I responded so readily to Peter's suggestion, but I must also take this opportunity to thank the many people who gave up so much of their time in order to reminisce about their past and present associations with me.

There must have been occasions when it could not have been too easy to look back with the fondest of memories, yet of one thing I am certain. Very few people can have come into contact with me without gaining some impression of the way I do business or enjoy myself. I have never been a negative sort of character, but I feel that I have ended up with far more friends than enemies.

This book is dedicated to my family, my close friends, my loyal staff and close colleagues over many years in the holiday industry and, above all, to the hundreds of thousands of people who have given their loyal support to the Pontin's holiday centres during a period of forty five years. Without them there would be no book, and certainly no happy life. Before listing those who have assisted with the research into the story of my life and times there can be only one message – 'Don't forget, book early!'

First of all, my wife Dorothy, my daughter Pat, my sister Elsie, and my brother Len. Others, in alphabetical order, were Ronnie Aitken, Derek Allwright, Mike Austin, John and Valerie Barnett,

Trevor Bailey, Percy Cansdale, Audrey Dean, David Gwyn, Trevor Hemmings, Joyce Hey, Eileen Langridge, Charles Laws, A.S. McLaren, Jeff Mallinson, George Mann, Ann Miller, Jimmy Perry, OBE, Derek Porter, Joe Rubido, Wally Riglar, George Ross Goobey, Walter Rowley, Albert Shirley, Bob Shilling, Peter Smith, Ed Sparrow, Eddie and Liz Stamper and Celia Wilson.

My thanks go out to everyone. If any name is missing I can assure you that it is entirely unintentional.


Whitehall Court, July 1991.

# FOREWORD

## By Jimmy Perry, joint creator of *Hi-De-Hi*

SOME years ago I was having a drink in the bar after a lodge meeting of the Grand Order of Water Rats, when my Brother Rat, Sir Fred, said to me: 'Jimmy your television series *Hi-De-Hi* has got it exactly right. I recognise every character'. I took this as a great compliment from a man who was one of the pioneers in giving working people holidays that they could afford.

Times were hard when Fred opened his first holiday camp in 1946. In spite of the fact that the war was over, food and most of life's essentials were strictly rationed. It was Fred, whose planning and initiative gave them holidays, that brought cheer into their lives.

Today the holiday business is a huge industry. Every summer airports are jammed as millions of people make for the sun. They take cheap package holidays for granted, but few of them realise it was Fred Pontin's foresight that led the way in the great British trek into the sun. He was the man who had the vision to see the enormous potential of package holidays abroad.

In 1963 he opened his first Pontinental Holiday Village in Sardinia. The price: £50 for two weeks holiday, including three meals a day and the flight. By 1979 Fred Pontin had built an empire of twenty-four holiday camps in the U.K. and ten Pontinental holiday villages and hotels abroad; giving over a million people a year holidays that twenty years before they could only have dreamed about.

Sir Fred's work for charity is a legend, raising money for so many causes. In 1968, as Chief Barker of the Variety Club of Great Britain, he raised over a million pounds for charity.

This is Sir Fred Pontin's own story, a man of vision whose motto was: 'Find out what the public wants and give it to them at a price they can afford'.

J.P.

# CONTENTS

*Chapter One*

# LIFE'S PAGEANT

BBC TV's light entertainment programme *HI-De-HI* attracted regular audiences of up to sixteen million viewers and I have to confess that I was one of them.

Watching the programme on a Sunday evening brought back many memories of the early days, and I was particularly intrigued by the fact that the entire concept of the series was based around the staff and not the holidaymakers, who, like absentee owner Joe Maplin, were never very much in evidence.

Previous programmes on life in post-war holiday camps were pathetic caricatures of the real thing. Tales of concentration camp atmospheres, being awakened by loudspeakers at the crack of dawn and the need to escape by digging under the perimeter fence were nothing more than corny music-hall jokes. It was refreshing, therefore, to see how David Croft and fellow Water Rat Jimmy Perry OBE captured the flavour of what went on behind the scenes – even though most of what was portrayed was grossly exaggerated.

This simply added to the entertainment value of the series, all episodes of which were subjected to repeat showings and, in the main, gave the fully justified impression that guests and the staff were all having a very good time.

Pontin's holiday camps have progressed immeasurably in terms of comfort and facilities over the years. I gain great satisfaction from the fact that today's Holiday Club Pontin's is under the control and organisation of some of the most experienced people in the business, most of whom, I must add, were selected and trained by me.

I mentioned *HI-De-HI* specifically because this programme served to remind me of the origins of my business and how it came to change not only my life but also the lives of thousands of people...members of my own family, the enormous numbers of staff who have worked in Pontin's and, above all, my guests, without whom there would have been no business and no happy times.

This book is about my own life and times, so it would do no harm to pause for a moment to reflect on not only what I have achieved but also just how fortunate I have been as a result of my entry into the business of making people happy.

If an ordinary chap from working-class origins can accompany Her Majesty The Queen's Consort to an evening meeting at a London greyhound track . . . if this same man can lead in his own racehorses after they had won the Grand National and Schweppes Gold Trophy in the same season . . . then for this rather unlikely fellow to cap it all by acting as chairman at a memorable celebratory dinner attended by no less than five British Prime Ministers, there must be a story worth the telling.

A derelict and war-scarred holiday camp could perhaps be described as an improbable foundation for the good fortune which lies behind such a tale, but that is where it all started. If there is to be any moral which could possibly be attached to this account of my extraordinary life it must be related to the maxim that no one should ever fail to make use of their experiences. Good, bad or just indifferent, these are certain to come in useful at some further stage in what the late Arthur Marshall described in his own autobiography as 'life's rich pageant'.

The creation of wealth can lead a person down many different paths, any one or even a combination of which could result in the destruction of that individual for what may be a variety of reasons. Wealth is capable of creating power and power can lead to corruption in one form or another.

Wealth creates access to all manner of material substances; wealth can be squandered, it can be abused and it can lead to self-destruction by the abuse of the material substances. For instance, how many times do we read of successful pop stars and possessors of inherited wealth succumbing to hard drugs which have become

available only because of the wealth of the individuals concerned?

How often do we learn that a wealthy person, so intoxicated with the sense of his own importance and infallibility, has taken just one chance too many and has seen his empire come crashing down around him?

These questions are posed to illustrate that the mere possession of wealth cannot automatically lead to the unique sequence of events described near the beginning of this narrative.

I am the first to admit that I have not led a blameless life, but I am noted for my staying power. What I have achieved has been as a result of being aware of my limitations, learning and benefiting from my varied experiences, not to mention the odd adventure, and also by recognising that there are many others who have not been so fortunate in the course of their own progress through life.

It has been said that some successful people make their own luck and I feel that I have have been blessed with the necessary confidence when adopting such an approach. Consistency and strength of purpose have also been common factors and I have always had a sense of determination to achieve the required result without suffering too much from feelings of despair.

There was, however, a time when I felt that the right opportunity was being denied to me and I must have come very close to pursuing my frustrated ambitions in a different direction.

It was early in the Spring of 1946 and I was driving a large open tourer, which had been shipped over to England from America during the war. My companion was a young secretary who knew the area.

I stopped for petrol at a filling station just south of Weston-Super-Mare feeling rather despondent. We were engaged upon what was fast proving to be an abortive search for readily available, de-requisitioned anti-aircraft or searchlight sites on or nearby the coast of Somerset. I had hit upon the idea of converting these types of property into holiday camps, a concept which had been developed on a national basis by people such as Billy Butlin and Captain Harry Warner in the 1930's.

Hostilities had ceased and, having been released from my wartime duties, I was anxious to fulfil my ambition to make a lot of money. I was then 40 years old. Before the war I had been working on the London Stock Exchange, but Hitler's activities had been an interruption, so I was intent upon making up for lost time.

Former members of the armed forces had their gratuities to

spend and were desperate for cheap family holidays, so I felt that if I moved quickly I could be among the leading contenders in that year's holiday season. This would be the first after six long years of hardship and sacrifice by the people of Great Britain.

I was not too ambitious in those early days. A small camp to cater for say fifty to sixty guests would provide a good start and get the cash flowing. There was no doubt that I knew what I wanted but the frustration was that I seemed to be getting nowhere in pursuit of my modest objective.

I asked the garage attendant if he knew of any likely sites, but he shook his head. It seemed that all local positions had been cleared by a large party of French workers, who had dismantled the redundant buildings and transported the materials back home. These could be reassembled in Caen to provide temporary housing for local people who had lost their homes during the fighting.

If, on the other hand, I would be interested in a pre-war, purpose-built holiday camp which had just been de-requisitioned by the Government . . . the garageman recommended that I should go and see a Leslie Dean. He lived just a few miles away in a village called Berrow near Burnham-on-Sea across the narrow roads which led to Brean Sands and beyond.

Although he was not to know it at the time, the garage attendant had just launched me on a career which was to result in my becoming a household name, known throughout the whole of the United Kingdom and even in the sunspots of Europe.

This single incident led to me becoming a millionaire and earning a knighthood for what people have described as my enthusiastic charitable activities.

*Chapter Two*

# EAST END DAYS

I HAVE always been proud of my Cockney origins, having been born in Shoreditch in the East End of London on 24th October 1906, though the family moved out to Walthamstow a few years later. In those days Walthamstow was considered to be a country area with much better surroundings for bringing up a growing family.

I was the eldest of six children and with the same names as my father, Frederick William. Being the eldest, throughout the whole of my adult life I suppose that I have tended to have a dominating influence on the rest of my kith and kin.

My father was a cabinet maker of some distinction, following an equally distinguished line from his father and the male members of two generations before him. My mother was absolutely devoted to her husband and children, most of whom became associated with me and my future business activities.

In common with my younger brothers, Harry and Len, I was educated at the local council school in Blackhorse Road, Walthamstow before moving on to become a fee-paying day pupil at St. George Monoux Grammar School, Walthamstow. I had another brother, Stanley, who died at the age of ten, the day after Len was born in 1918. My sisters Florrie and Elsie also took advantage of the good educational opportunities made available by our parents.

Len has now assumed the role of family historian. Because I have been subject to a vast amount of publicity over the years I have received many letters from people who claimed some form of family relationship, mostly for what were obviously pecuniary reasons.

5

Very few were able to provide any evidence of the alleged connection, though on one occasion a very genuine letter arrived from a distant cousin in Australia and this prompted my brother to follow up some of the leads which were provided from this source.

As a result we now have a detailed family tree dating back to John Pontin, who was born in 1793. It is thought that the Pontin family came over from Normandy in the Seventeenth Century, but Len has much more work to do before we shall have a fuller picture of our ancestors. We do know, however, that my father's role as a cabinet maker goes a long way back. A George Pontin, born 1812 in Bethnal Green, was described as a cabinet maker in the parish records.

One of my earlier memories is of my mother rushing down to the railway station at Blackhorse Road, Walthamstow every night of the week to meet father when he returned from his place of work in Shoreditch. While my brothers and sisters were growing up I was expected to take on a position of some responsibility looking after the family. I had a regular evening routine, which allowed my parents to enjoy the odd drink at the Royal Standard public house on their way home to put the younger children to bed before sitting down to enjoy their evening meal.

My family has always been very close and we all made a frequent habit of calling in to see Grandma Belcher. She was my maternal grandmother, who had been widowed at a very young age. Her second husband, Tom Belcher, was a door-to-door collector for a coal merchant, but in the evenings he played the cornet with the orchestra at the very popular Collins Music Hall. Among the stars there was the cheeky comedian Max Miller, who would become a friend of mine during the course of my future career in the holiday camp industry.

Most weekends Tom Belcher would also be playing with two other musicians at the Royal Standard. He spent his last years as my guest at the South Devon Holiday Camp at Paignton, where he enjoyed watching the various outdoor sporting activities as well as the billiards matches played there in those days.

My parents were very much involved with the Walthamstow Avenue Football Club, an amateur football team which earned a national reputation as a result of their successes in the FA Cup.

Father and mother were enthusiastic supporters and took part in a wide variety of the club's activities. Their interest in the team was also shared by the entire family and it soon led to me becoming the club's treasurer and also their Press reporter. My match reports were regular features in the *Walthamstow Guardian*, the local newspaper.

In those days all of the players were officially described as amateurs and this status would have been compromised if they accepted payment for playing for the club. On the other hand, everyone who supported Walthamstow Avenue wanted success, so the club had to recruit footballers who were ready to exploit their superior talents for pecuniary purposes.

'Expenses', a euphemism for regular wages, were paid to members of the team and I became involved in all sorts of cash-raising activities to finance this extra-curricular, but very necessary activity. I organised the running of a tea and coffee bar, as well as selling programmes, to generate the necessary funds paid to the players in various surreptitious ways.

The other local amateur football club was Walthamstow Grange and there was great rivalry between the two clubs. I remember a preliminary round in the FA Cup when the teams were drawn against each other and the Avenue, playing at home, were a player short. I managed to recruit Jim Lewis, who eventually captained England as an amateur player. Lewis had an outstanding match on the left wing, scoring seven or eight goals in a 13-0 win for Avenue. He later joined Chelsea as a professional and his son, also played for the South West London club.

I very much wanted to be involved with the best amateur team in England, so I had no hesitation in working tirelessly, and enthusiastically for the club.

The family's enthusiasm for the Avenue club was undoubtedly generated by the fact that virtually every match seemed to have the atmosphere of a cup tie. Every opposing team wanted to beat the Avenue and this brought out the best in the players.

There seemed to be a never-ending series of celebrations as we saw the club earn promotion from the Spartan League into the Athenian League and eventually to the Isthmian League. My recollection is that the team was top of the league every year. This was a source of great delight to me, because nothing can be more rewarding than success in a competitive environment, regardless of whether it be of a business or sporting nature.

I also recall when Walthamstow Avenue reached the Third Round of the FA Cup. They were drawn away to Manchester United after beating Stockport County and Reading in the First and Second Rounds. The game was drawn with a goal each, a result which disappointed the fans who had travelled up from London. Groves, the centre forward, missed an open goal ten minutes from full time.

The replay could not be staged on Avenue's pitch and at the same time satisfy all of the two sides' many supporters, so it was arranged for the match to take place on Arsenal's ground at Highbury. Crowd capacity at Avenue was 12,000, but they seldom had less than 5,000 spectators, reflecting very well on the entertaining football played by this successful amateur club.

The match took place at Highbury on the following Wednesday afternoon before a crowd of 55,000 wildly enthusiastic spectators, most of whom were from the East End of London. Avenue lost by three goals to two in an exciting match which I shall never forget.

Bearing in mind that Manchester United ended the season as champions of the First Division of the Football League, Avenue's performance could be considered as very impressive and it gave us all a lift.

It is sad that such a fine amateur football club is no longer in existence. Avenue's ground is now a residential housing estate and, as a result of a merger between several clubs in the area, football is now represented by Redbridge Forest, a team which plays in the Premier Division of the Vauxhall League and competes in the annual FA Challenge Trophy.

Walthamstow Grange subsequently closed down as an active football team when their ground became a greyhound racing venue.

My interest in sport was undoubtedly kindled at St George Monoux Grammar School, where I not only took part in boxing matches – suffering a broken nose – but I also won the Victor Ludorum Cup by winning every sporting event available to me as a junior.

My brother Len reminds me that I also went on to win open events where I had to compete against the more senior pupils.

The cup has now been returned to the school, together with the photograph which recorded my success. This was framed in a very professional way by my father and both cup and framed photograph are now exhibited in the school's museum set up in 1977 after their 450th anniversary celebrations. Accompanied by brother Len, I had the honour to attend the event as chief guest.

The school provided a very good education. Former pupils include a High Court judge, numerous chartered accountants, stockbrokers and high-ranking bank officials.

Looking back, I feel that I did not reap the full benefit from my studies at St George Monoux Grammar School. I attribute this to the time lost when I had a form of nervous breakdown following the death of my young brother Stanley, to whom I was very close.

His death at the tender age of 10 was a great shock and I was sent away to Clacton-on-Sea to recuperate. As a result I missed the greater part of my first term at grammar school. Although I was always near the top of the class and in constant competition with two other pupils – Ashton, who subsequently qualified as chartered accountant and Hughes, who became a tea planter – I feel that I never really caught up with them.

I was always somewhat behind in some of the more important subjects, such as English and French, but I shall always be thankful that I am lucky enough to have an aptitude for figures, if not for all of the finer points of mathematics.

Looking retrospectively I suppose that I did reasonably well, given the circumstances, but I have always tended to set my standards very high. Second best has never really been good enough. My memories of St George Monoux include the name of the headmaster, Wally Topliss, who was stone deaf, but, as all mischievous new pupils soon learned to their cost, he was an expert at lip-reading!

I completed my schooling when I was not much more than 15 years of age, but, despite my above-average performance in the classroom I left without any educational qualifications. The pressing need was to earn money for the family, not to stay on in an effort to matriculate.

I was conscious of the fact that my parents had made many sacrifices over the years to give each of their children a good start in life, even though the cost of providing higher education was beyond their limited resources.

It should be borne in mind that I was just eight-years-old when the Great War started and my parents also had to provide for three other children. By the time I left school the family had grown to seven and my father was not able to work on a self-employed basis during the long period of hostilities.

He was a gifted and very skilled craftsman, but his war work was with Waring & Gillow, the furniture manufacturers, who were directed into the business of making wooden aircraft frames for both fighters and bombers being flown in combat by the Royal Flying Corps. This job – as important as it was - did not pay as well as making, restoring and repairing fine furniture for some of the grandest houses in England. It was important, therefore, that I should make a contribution to the family's income at the earliest opportunity.

*Incidentally, I came across an interesting little item of family history during the course of carrying out research for this book. Bob Shilling, who now runs his own travel agency business in West London, worked for me for many years. When his father died Bob inherited some woodworking tools which were originally in the ownership of his grandfather, who was also a cabinet-maker at Waring & Gillow at the time my own father worked there many years ago.*

*Among the beautifully-kept tools was a spirit-level made from wood and brass bearing the initials FWP, carved very neatly on the side of the instrument. Bob was not aware that my father had even been a cabinet-maker, let alone having worked for Waring & Gillow, but when he heard me talk about his skills on a national radio programme he contacted me and very generously returned the essential element of the cabinet-maker's craft to the family where he felt it belonged. A very charming gesture and I trust you will agree a remarkable coincidence.*

*If Bob's grandfather had borrowed the spirit-level from my father around 1910 I suppose the fact that it has been returned after all these years goes to show that there must be hope for the rest of us who are still awaiting the return of garden shears, books or other items loaned to neighbours and friends!*

My father wanted me to take up a career in banking and offered to arrange an interview with the Midland Bank. I was adamant that I did not have the slightest interest in following a career which relied upon I what I considered to be dead men's shoes.

I made it clear that it was the London Stock Exchange which had the most attraction as far as I was concerned. This was the place where fortunes were made. With the immense benefit of retrospective thought I would venture to suggest that my attitude at this time was probably influenced by the wild, almost hysterical, boom which took place in the investment markets during the post-war period of 1919-1920.

These exciting events must have been in my mind when discussing what career I would follow. I clearly remember telling my father that I wanted 'to become a millionaire'. I must have explained that it was impossible to make this sort of money working for a bank. Banks were places to keep your fortune, not to make it, at least as far as I was concerned in those early days.

Even at such a tender age, and with no direct knowledge of the workings of the City of London, I knew just what I wanted to do. I got my own way, despite my father's misgivings regarding the uncertainties connected with something which he did not really understand.

I had long been an avid reader of the financial columns of the national press and I was certain that the Stock Exchange was where all of the wealthy people had made their money by trading in stocks and shares, commodities and all manner of exciting pieces of paper. The City, I decided, was for me.

*Chapter Three*

# SOMETHING IN THE CITY

AS WAS USUAL in those times, it was a family connection which provided the introduction to a Mr Smith, who was employed as an office manager at a firm of gilt-edged jobbers called Gordon Askew and Biddough.

There was no time to enjoy the summer holidays that year, for it was the Monday following my last day at school that I reported to the firm's premises in the City of London.

I had been there for only one week – doing very little and spending most of my time sitting with the messengers – when I was called over by Mr Smith. He handed me a one pound note for my wages, then broke the news that he was sorry but he was instructed to give me, his newest clerk, just one week's notice. I found it difficult to understand what was happening and asked what I had done to deserve the sack.

The office manager told me not to worry, nothing was held against me, but the firm, which had a staff of 80, was going into liquidation. My immediate reaction was to return the money with the remark that perhaps the firm was going to need it more than me . . . Mr Smith laughed, then explained that it was to be a voluntary liquidation, purely for tax reasons.

It appeared that firms were taxed upon average earnings over a period of three years. Askews had enjoyed two very good years and voluntary liquidation was a perfectly legal and common tax avoidance device in those days.

Mr Smith seemed to be treating the whole matter very lightly. He announced, to my great relief, that I would have no trouble in finding a similar job with another firm. He further astonished me by saying that I would qualify for a bonus – the lowest on offer, but of a sum of no less than £100. A considerable amount of money in those days.

So, after only two weeks of employment in the world of high finance, I was to receive (even I could not say it had really been earned) the magnificent sum of £102. It may not have proved to be a fortune, but it did make a jolly good start.

I couldn't wait to get home in order to tell my parents this splendid news. As far as I am concerned, my love of money started from that wonderful summer's day in 1921 . . . and the feeling has never left me.

When I took up my job with Askews I was dressed in my grandfather's long, double-breasted jacket, which my mother had altered to match the latest trend in men's fashion. I soon learned that it was important to look the part, having seen the smart clothes worn by the partners and senior employees, so I had no hesitation in deciding to invest some of my newly-acquired wealth in a brand new outfit.

Hector Powe in Bishopsgate was a tailor's shop of some distinction as far as I was concerned, so I graced them with a visit. I spent over £40 on an off-the-peg black jacket, striped trousers, hat, suede gloves, spats and rolled umbrella. I was now ready to face the world and my new employers.

These turned out to be Messrs Gow and Parsons, a newly-formed firm of stockbrokers seeking five senior clerks and two juniors. One of the juniors was to be me. The other was Walpole, a lad of 14 years of age who had one week's seniority over me because I was the last member of the staff to be recruited to the new business.

The senior partners were John Barnett Gow, who came to London from a firm in Glasgow called Gow Brothers and Gemmell, and a Mr Parsons, who was previously with a firm of merchant bankers I remember as Lathan & Roselli. Both partners employed their sons in their latest commercial enterprise. Albert Parsons was in charge of 'names' clients and Ian Gow had similar duties in a basement in Throgmorton Street, close to the floor of the Stock Exchange.

I was given what I have always described as an 'Irishman's rise'. My wages were fixed at fifteen shillings per week (75 pence in decimal currency). Walpole and myself had a routine which involved the daily collection of official and unofficial lists of share prices from the printers, who I clearly remember provided a very erratic service.

The Stock Exchange ceased trading at 3.30 in the afternoon and five o'clock was when the lists should have become available. More often than not, however, I had to hang around until 7 p.m. before I could rush back to the office and prepare to post the information to the provincial brokers, for whom my employers were conducting regular dealing business on their behalf on the floor of the Stock Exchange.

These out-of-town brokers relied upon the lists in order to keep their clients in touch with the London share markets.

All should have been well except that the other junior and young Pontin were often at loggerheads about whose turn it was to be doing this menial, but important, daily task. The inevitable happened. Neither of us did the post one day, and to compound our misdemeanours the office was left with the lights on and the doors wide open.

We were given the sack. I started to appreciate that fortunes were not all that easily made in the City. Keeping a steady job was proving to be a difficult task.

Perhaps junior clerks were difficult to recruit, so whatever the reason, we were both reinstated by Albert Parsons, though I was determined that I was not going back to do the junior job. I succeeded in being promoted to the task of assisting the son of one of the partners, who was then a red button clerk on the floor of the Stock Exchange.

My duties consisted of handling 'names', registering details of buyers and sellers of shares. I had, at last, been given a job which gave me an insight into the deals conducted in the share markets.

I began to understand terminology such as 'bulls', 'bears', 'stags', highs and lows and middle market prices. Dividends, dividend cover, yields, price earnings ratios, capital issues – all of these terms became very familiar with my keenness to digest every scrap of information on offer.

I must have performed my duties in a satisfactory manner, because I was rewarded with a ten shillings rise bringing my weekly wages up to 25 shillings. Further increments followed and I was soon earning twice this amount.

I continued to be very ambitious. It must have showed, because I soon graduated to jobbers ledger, a cash book record of transactions between jobbers and brokers. This promotion did not come without some prior jiggery-pokery, mainly on the basis that I thought that the man whom I eventually succeeded was far from efficient and had been promoted over my head. I was certain that I could do the job better. I bitterly resented the fact that the office manager had favoured the other person and would not listen to my urgent protestations.

A showdown was soon brought about when I contrived to 'find' some names which appeared to have been 'mislaid' by the party I thought was an incompetent incumbent as far as the much-coveted job was concerned.

I should perhaps explain that the direct effect of my employers not being able to pass on the names of the buyers of shares to the selling brokers was that the other firm then had the right to 'sell out' the holdings for cash to a market jobber. As a result, Gow and Parsons were forced to finance any losses on the deals from their own resources.

In due course I was to receive the much-sought-after promotion and a rise in my weekly wage to four pounds ten shillings. The office manager was eventually sacked when the partners came to appreciate that I had been treated very unfairly.

Before not too much time had passed there was what I should perhaps describe as a form of poetic justice. When I was employed on the clients ledger I made a very serious error in mixing up the statements of account which were sent out to a father and son, both of whom had been dealing – with the benefit of insider knowledge – in the shares of a sugar refining company.

My slip-up caused a hell of a row. Both clients wrote and complained to the senior partner and demanded that I should be sacked! I was given one month's notice.

I had been with the firm for over four years, so the consolation was that I had gained some very valuable experience. Luckily I had enough commonsense to take a realistic view in that, given the particular circumstances, the dismissal was undoubtedly justified. Although I considered that I had been entitled to take matters into my own hands on the earlier occasion, when I felt that my work had lacked proper recognition from the office manager, I did not see how I could possibly resent dismissal for what can only be described as incompetence.

In later years, when I was running my own business and dealing with large numbers of staff, I considered it essential that I should always be in a position to be able to justify any disciplinary action which was proved to be necessary and I sought similar realism from any transgressors.

Out of a job and with the share markets relatively quiet after the industrial and rubber booms which followed the First World War, I approached the Stock Exchange Benevolent Fund, which acted as a type of employment agency. They directed me to Bristow Brothers, a firm of stock jobbers who were the third largest in foreign stocks. I must have impressed them at my interview by my knowledge and the extent of my experience, so I was offered a salaried clerical position at an annual salary £500 – subject to a good reference from my previous employer.

Bearing in mind the enforced nature of my departure, I was more than a little apprehensive when I called on the new office manager at Gow & Parsons. I need not have worried. Despite the circumstances of my leaving I was given a reference which was good enough to secure my new position with Bristow Brothers.

I was again employed on the jobbers ledger, where the volume of work did not reach any appreciable level until after the firm's partners returned from the floor of the Stock Exchange after 3.30 in the afternoon. It was then necessary to write up all of the transactions conducted during the day's business.

I remember the leisurely lunches and games of dominoes at J. Lyons' premises in Throgmorton Street while other clerks and myself waited for the partners and dealers to return to their offices.

I also learned new aspects of the business in stocks and shares, in that my employers were involved with arbitrage, the traffic in securities in order to take advantage of different prices in other markets. Most of Bristows' foreign transactions were conducted on the markets in Belgium, where bearer shares, as opposed to registered stocks, were the predominant feature.

I broadened the depth of my experience and knowledge, but, once I had assimilated and understood the precise nature of the day to day transactions, I began to find the work rather boring and far from inspirational.

I was in no position to create and accumulate capital of my own, though, at least, I was learning how sterling and foreign currencies were being converted into paper and how this paper represented wealth, power and influence.

After a year with Bristows I felt I was in a rut. Something had to be done about it. There I was earning a reasonable salary, with bonuses of about £100, but I felt that it was time to move on.

At least on this occasion, my projected move was not being forced upon me, so around about my twenty first birthday I returned to the Stock Exchange Benevolent Fund to see if they could find me a better job with improved prospects.

Perhaps they felt that I warranted some form of challenge, because they ignored the conventional broking and jobbing houses and introduced me to a company called Rock Investments Limited, which was operated by Martin Coles Harman.

I met the man from whom I was to learn more about the creation of wealth from quoted securities in the form of 'paper' transactions than from all of my previous employers put together. It was a move that led me into a phase of my City career that was to have a profound influence on my future success, though I could never have known it at the time.

Harman was famous, or perhaps notorious, for owning Lundy Island situated off the coast of Devon in the Bristol Channel. He had entertained ambitions to declare some form of independence and create a tax haven on the lines of Jersey and Guernsey in the Channel Islands, but the authorities would have none of it.

Although it was contrary to British Law he went as far as to introduce his own currency, the bronze coins of which were called puffins and half-puffins, after the sea birds on the island. They also bore his portrait making him one of the few private individuals ever to achieve this status.

The Government were not amused, but only a nominal fine was imposed upon him in 1930. Souvenir sets of the offending coins were struck in 1965 from Harman's original dies. He also produced and sold Lundy postage stamps. This time there was no protest from the authorities and subsequent owners of the island have followed this practice.

His efforts created only modest returns for this enterprising and innovative businessman with whom I soon formed a good working relationship. In due course it could perhaps be said that I became his protégé and formed a great deal of respect for his business acumen.

Because of this I have never had any difficulty in being even-handed regarding Harman's eventual fall from grace, and his subsequent prison sentence, which resulted from charges of fraudulent transactions in stocks and shares.

At the time of my arrival in the City Harman was controlling and operating a series of companies with grand sounding names, such as London Irish Trust, Oceana Consolidated and the British

Bank for Foreign Trade. They we re all dealing with each other as a method of keeping up the prices of various stocks and shares in which Harman's investment companies were interested.

I came to be very much involved with the entire process, which I can only describe as "dog eating dog". This type of activity certainly appeared to be legal in those days, when controls were not nearly as stringent as they are in the scandal-hit 1990s.

I had my preliminary job interview with the office manager, Dickie Doyle, who figured very prominently in my post-war business activities. He became acting chairman of Pontin's Limited when I became incapacitated as a result of a serious motoring accident.

I was offered an annual salary of £800, which Harman immediately increased to £1,000 as soon as he realised the full extent of my considerable experience. By the mid-1930s my annual earnings increased to some £2,000, but I was expected to work very hard and not question the long hours which were required by my new employer.

I have often reflected that if I had joined the Midland Bank on leaving school I would have been very lucky to have earned anything approaching this level of salary. Moreover, I would have been institutionalised to such an extent that my success and enthusiasm would have been lost to an important sector of the British holiday and leisure industries.

My duties were far from routine. At the age of 26 I was dealing on a basis which I found both exciting and stimulating. As my experience became broadened I also gained increased confidence and learned to think for myself. So much so that at a later date I was able to warn Harman of the markedly dubious manner in which certain of his associates were conducting their activities in a series of stock transactions.

In doing so I earned my employer's respect and also what I hoped would be his admiration for spotting the blatant attempt at deception. To say that I have never held any ill will against Martin Coles Harman is to understate the case.

During the course of my employment with his organisation I learned virtually every facet of the capital markets.

Although my employer's career was to be ruined, I was able to take advantage of the opportunity to learn about finance by first-hand experience. When, in due course, I was to conceive an idea for a business which required capital investment, as opposed to an over-reliance on borrowed money, it was my former City connections which were to provide the means for the creation of my outstandingly successful business empire.

*Chapter Four*

# CHAMPAGNE DAYS

I MARRIED in 1929, having met my wife, Dorothy Mortimer, at one of the social events organised at Walthamstow Avenue Football Club.

We were blessed with a daughter, Patricia Heather Mavis, who was born in November 1937. I did not have a lot of say in the choice of two of these names but I felt that Heather might bring us all some luck.

Being accustomed to annual earnings of up to £2,000, but now having increased family responsibilities, there was a pressing need to generate more income. I had no capital to invest as a partner in another City firm and I could not face the prospect of working as just another inconsequential employee.

Having experienced entrepreneurial enterprise when working with Martin Coles Harman, I felt that the time had come to start my own business. The question which faced me was what could I do to earn a worthwhile return without the need to invest capital?

Football pools were in their infancy, having been started by Littlewoods and Vernons. I decided to try my hand by setting up Smiths Soccer Totes Limited. Premises were obtained in Bride Lane, Ludgate Circus, very close to a boxing gymnasium where Primo Carnera was training for a title fight.

I bought a mailing list containing 20,000 names and I recruited some part-time employees as well as members of my family to send fixed-odds coupons to addresses all over the United Kingdom. There was a covering letter which intimated that the prospective customers had been recommended by 'reliable clients'.

This exercise in direct marketing proved to be reasonably successful. Turnover soon increased to an acceptable level and I was starting to earn some money again. I introduced various combinations such as 'four draws' and 'seven home wins' so that altogether there were seven separate pools.

Although I was not fully aware of the implications at that time, my clients were actually being offered a degree of what amounted to 'illegal' credit, which proved to be an advantage over the larger companies, who could not afford to anticipate an impending decision on a gambling case in the High Court.

Unfortunately, my customers tended to offer payment in settlement of their accounts only when they won and not when they lost. Business could not continue to operate on such an uncertain basis. My description of this experience has always been "Skinners – No Winners" – I fixed the odds according to the number of "skinners" and took the chance of getting paid.

Other pools were formed and I was joined in this burgeoning business by my sister Elsie. I diversified into bookmaking and life became less precarious until the outbreak of war put an end to horse racing.

Hitler did not strike though before I benefited from some twelve months of relative prosperity. I had many regular clients, including John Cobb, the racing motorist, with whom I shared a regular bottle of Veuve Clicquot champagne at El Vino in Leadenhall Street. When Elsie talks about the old days, and this time in particular, she is inclined to say 'You didn't do too bad'.

She was right. Life was very tolerable. I was my own boss and I had some cash in my pocket. This form of activity was not likely to lead to everlasting prosperity, but, in any event, King and country had other plans for me and there was to be a dramatic fall in my standard of living.

I had suffered from deafness in one ear for many years so, as far as the Services were concerned, this was a disability which excluded me from active duties in the war against Adolf.

I went to the appropriate authorities to register my availability for other work in the war effort and I was directed to the Orkney Islands, where I was instructed to report to the catering manager. He was responsible for feeding what ultimately proved to be an enormous workforce, many of whose members were to be mustered from the Republic of Ireland.

I had only recently been recruited as a reserve policeman and had reported to Mincing Lane in the City to collect an armlet, truncheon and helmet. I should also have reported to the Guildhall in order to be sworn in, but, after an altogether too-festive an evening with some of my bookmaking friends at the Trocadero restaurant and a Soho night club, I overslept and missed this solemn occasion.

One of my colleagues had, however, completed all of the necessary formalities and one of his first duties on that same night was to guard Southwark bridge. This was a far from pleasant task in November 1939, being cold and damp and thoroughly unattractive.

I decided that this was no way to spend the winter nights. The posting to the Orkneys presented an opportunity to escape from the duties of a glorified air raid warden, even though I had never heard of the islands, let alone knew where to find them. I had some previous experience as a special constable during the General Strike of 1926 and, although my memories of those days were far from disagreeable, they were not to change my mind about the move northwards.

Rail warrant in my pocket, I caught the 3.30 p.m. train from Euston on the first leg of my journey to the Orkney Islands. By then I had a vague notion of where these islands lay in geographical terms. On arrival at Thurso the next day, in the company of two other luckless souls, I found a local hotel where we could spend the night.

Our first task was to escort 40 Irish labourers on the ferry ship to the islands, the southernmost of which lay just a few miles off the North West coast of the Scottish mainland. It so happened that I was dressed in my 'City uniform' of black jacket, striped trousers, spats and a trilby hat.

Our ferry ship travelled to Stromness and Hoy escorted by a Royal Naval frigate. When we were told that the Pentland Firth was swarming with enemy submarines I began to wonder whether or not Southwark Bridge would have afforded a more attractive proposition.

We were eventually put ashore on a jetty overlooking Scapa Flow. It was in very poor condition, not having been repaired since it was damaged in World War One and, needless to say, the weather was entirely predictable. A blizzard made the landing even more hazardous so we were not impressed by this inauspicious welcome.

Neither were we reassured by the state of the roads and the open lorries which were to transport our party to the accommodation site. All of the workmen were carrying their belongings in brown paper parcels or carrier bags, and when the lorries sank up to their axles in thick brown mud their possessions had to be temporarily discarded in order to push the vehicles on to firmer ground.

My rather superior outfit appeared to single me out as a cut above the others in terms of sartorial elegance and I managed to exclude myself from such a strenuous and thoroughly messy activity.

We arrived at the accommodation camp, which was being constructed for the Admiralty by Balfour Beatty. My own quarters consisted of a little room measuring six-feet by ten feet six inches. There were no items of furniture other than an iron bedstead, a flock mattress and a pillow. There were a few blankets but no sheets and no pillow case.

I lost no time in complaining to Mr Sharpe, the site agent, on the basis that I was certainly not accustomed to such primitive accommodation and I would not stand for it. It was no surprise that I received the classic reply of 'Don't you know there's a bloody war on!'. I knew then that my hitherto comfortable lifestyle was to change on quite a dramatic basis.

This was the time of the 'phoney war', but as far as I was concerned privation was to commence from that day onward. It was to be a long time before my life was to return to some form of normality.

My immediate superior, the catering manager, was soon the victim of a nervous breakdown so I was called upon to take over his duties. The living conditions of the construction workers could only be described as horrific. I was charged with the responsibility of feeding them on a weekly budget of one pound seven shillings and six pence (£1.37) for each person.

The numbers in the workforce eventually built up to 15,000 and this became my first experience of mass catering. As well as the Irish there were Norwegians from Stavanger.

All supplies were subject to the rationing regulations, so I made use of every conceivable device in an effort to provide a balanced diet, despite the limited nature of the menus. I remember buying excellent beef cattle 'on the hoof' at Kirkwall and there were also plentiful supplies of eggs in the islands. Not all of the raw material was up to these standards and I soon came to rely upon the ingenuity of the cooks to make the grub more palatable to my ever-ravenous workers.

Some of my readers may now be able judge for themselves whether or not these early experiences were to have a beneficial effect on feeding the guests at my holiday camps opened just after the war ended and in conditions where the rationing of food was to remain with us for almost ten years.

The workforce was building oil container and dummy ships as well as accommodation units. They attracted numerous reconnaissance flights by German aircraft, which were sometimes followed by enemy air attacks. It appeared that the allied efforts to convince the Germans that our naval forces were greater than they actually were proved to be successful.

When an air raid killed three of my workers I grew to understand that there could be no guarantee of survival – even in such a remote outpost of the United Kingdom.

It was at this time that I was fortunate to meet a person who has played a very significant role in my personal life as well as what was to be my post-war business career in the holiday camp industry. Ann Calder Scott Miller, who was then 24 years of age, was employed by the Civil Service as the Food Executive Officer for the Orkney and Shetland Islands. It was necessary for me to have to deal with her in connection with rations for the construction workers.

She was also the National Registration Officer with the duties of keeping personal records on the entire population of the islands, both indigenous and migrant.

Ann Miller was educated in the Orkney Islands and Edinburgh University, where she graduated with a M.A. and B. Com. Before the war she had spent a year with the John Lewis Partnership in London at their Oxford Street store under a graduate training scheme. She was seeking commercial experience in order to complement her degree qualifications.

The outbreak of hostilities took her back to her parents' home in the Orkneys, where her mother had applied for the civil service job on her behalf, even though Ann was very keen to join the Women's Royal Air Force and play her part in the war. Her father, a lighthouse keeper, would not countenance such a spirit of adventure so her wartime duties were confined to registration formalities and being responsible for controlling civilian and military food supplies.

Life was never conducted on a wholly routine basis in the storm-battered islands, but Ann Miller, being a local girl and having many friends, was able to introduce me to many social activities that were a pleasant divergence from life in the accommodation camp. Summers were short, but on the few days when there was no wind and the sun shone, we obtained a brief release from our onerous and tedious duties. We'd enjoy the scenery together, trying to forget that there was a war on.

The austerity of my life in the Orkneys was to be relieved to a considerable extent by my close relationship with Ann Miller. I am pleased to record that this cannot be described in such hackneyed terms as 'just another wartime romance'. It was also the start of a personal and business relationship which has endured over a period of some 50 years, up to and including the present day. Her name will figure prominently in this record of my life.

I left the Orkney Islands just after the Germans surrendered in May 1945. I was still of military age so there was no question of my being able to return to normal civilian life. Because of my wartime experience I was directed to a National Service Hostel at Coventry where I was to receive a week's training before being sent to undertake managerial responsibilities at a similar establishment elsewhere in the United Kingdom.

My tuition was cut short when news was received of a riot at the Government's original hostel for manual workers at Jubilee Drive, Kidderminster, an accommodation unit of chalets for 950 male forge workers and 50 female land girls from nearby sugar beet fields. The manager, a retired colonel, had been there for only three weeks before being forced to pack in the job after he had been physically assaulted. He could no longer stand the strain of trying to keep the inmates under some form of acceptable control.

I was ordered to go to Kidderminster the next day. I had already arranged to take Ann Miller to the theatre to see *Arsenic and Old Lace* so I managed to delay my appointment until the last day of the week. Ann had broken her journey at Coventry on her way to an appointment in London with Lord Woolton, the Food Minister, to discuss her future employment in the Civil Service.

I was not given any details of the riot and the manager's forced departure from Kidderminster, so I arrived at the hostel in a state of complete ignorance as far as its grim reputation was concerned. I soon became aware, though, of the hostility that was extended to people with any degree of authority.

The staff, including the catering officer, entertainments manager, matron and nursing sisters, took me on a tour of the site. In the assembly hall I was the first to notice a crudely written poster bearing the text 'Welcome to the new manager' under the insignia of the skull and crossbones.

That night, after members of the camp's population returned from the local pubs (alcoholic liquor not being available on the site) there was another riot with fighting between many of the men, missiles being thrown and fire hoses played on the staff and inmates alike. I quickly retreated to a bungalow which had been allocated as my personal living quarters.

Having carefully locked all of the doors, I prepared a plan for dealing with the situation. I thought that I had not come through the war just to be intimidated by a crowd of ruffians.

There was clearly a case for me to make my presence felt before I suffered the same fate as my predecessor. Next morning I went to see the person in charge of the local office of the Ministry of Labour. I announced to this astonished official that I was going to get rid of the main rabble rousers so that some degree of discipline could be restored in the camp.

Matters could not be allowed to continue on the existing basis. The drunken festivities were causing nothing but mayhem as far as the manager's position was concerned. It was to be a question of if they did not go, I certainly would.

I was told that I would be very unwise to carry out such a policy as the men were engaged upon work of national importance involving the manufacture of weapons and ammunition. I am pleased to say, however, that I was successful in getting my own way in the matter.

I warned the local police that I was sacking about twenty troublemakers and that they had better be on hand to supervise the arrangements, which ran the risk of violence. There was indeed a police presence when I dismissed the now sober ringleaders. There were the inevitable protests but I made it clear that my decision was final. There were to be no second chances under my new regime.

Perhaps my height of six feet three inches and a heavy frame had something to do with it, but I got away with this course of action and I enjoyed a large whisky when it was all over.

These measures were not welcomed by Cadburys' management, who were responsible for the site. They complained of the 'oppressive conduct' of the new administrator. My response was to insist that as I was the ninth manager in four and a half years there was clearly a need for a new approach to discipline. If they did not support my policy then they had better start looking for number ten.

I got my own way again and, although the remainder of my stay was far from uneventful, I did at least last the course. I improved the living conditions and the quality of the food, as well as the entertainment . . . and took the precaution of having a bodyguard accompanied by an alsatian dog.

I still had problems. Some of the workers stole my car and abandoned it with housebreaking tools in Kidderminster. Then I had trouble from American servicemen mixing with the land girls causing racial tensions between the black and white GI's who attended dances at the hostel.

Looking back I feel that my experience at Kidderminster was to stand me in good stead for my future career in mass catering and entertainment at the post-war holiday camps.The establishment of these camps was to change not only my own life, but that of Ann Miller and the lives of all members of my family.

*Chapter Five*

# WELCOME CAMPERS!

I WAS constantly seeking a release from Kidderminster, and when this was granted I joined forces with the site's catering manager, a man called Youlton. The rebuilding of Bristol offered opportunities for exploiting our wartime experience, so, after seeing the local authority, we tendered for the operation of a former 1,000 bed camp at Bedminster.

The council had imported large numbers of workers for the reconstruction programme. Unlike Kidderminster, our partnership could operate this camp on a commercial basis, with the council paying a fee for our services. We entered into a fifty-fifty profit sharing arrangement with me providing the initial cash capital of £100 and Youlton the catering equipment that got us into business.

This was never likely to be a highly profitable venture, but it was a re-introduction to the spirit of free enterprise and capitalism. The Stock Exchange had not returned to anything like the pre-war level of trading, so my immediate future did not lie in that direction. Throughout the whole of post-war Britain money was scarce and businesses now being released from their wartime activities were only just starting to think about peacetime trading and the manufacture of consumer goods.

My ideas for the provision of 'value for money' family holidays were taking shape. I needed a suitable site to make a start before too many other people came to the same conclusion . . . and my search led me to the front door of Leslie Dean's house near Burnham-on-Sea, Somerset.

It would not be too difficult to imagine what was passing through my mind when I parked my car outside his house. There were fine views across the Somerset Levels to Brent Knoll and the Mendip Hills, home of the famous Cheddar Caves and Burrington Combe, which provided inspiration for the well known 19th century hymn *Rock of Ages*.

A fine sandy beach stretching over seven miles from Burnham-on-Sea to Brean Down was only a very short distance away and the Brean Sands site, which had been recommended by the petrol pump attendant, was just down the road. This was an attractive area for holidays and no mistake.

What's more, the coast of North Somerset was easily accessible from the highly populated areas in the West Midlands and Bristol. There were main line Great Western Railway Stations at Weston-super-Mare and the nearby market town of Highbridge. Trains also ran direct from Paddington in Central London.

Much of Britain's coastline had been out of bounds during the war years and my considered view was that this would provide an added incentive to those seeking a break from an austere peacetime. Because of the intervention of the war, paid holidays were still a novelty after the passing of the Holidays with Pay Act in 1938, which gave all employees an entitlement to a week's paid leave, together with the usual public holidays.

I came to the conclusion that gratuities being paid to ex-servicemen would also fuel a demand for places in holiday camps that was sure to exceed supply. I could not wait to put my theories to the ultimate test – the ownership of a seaside holiday centre.

I had been somewhat dismayed when seeing 'my' site for the first time. Many of the wooden huts had been badly damaged when the US army had taken part in a little fun with their tanks before they quit the place just before the Normandy landings. They had been training for the invasion by carrying out exercises on the nearby beach, which resembled those in Northern France.

I took the view that some form of compensation would be payable by the Government and perhaps this could be part of the deal. If there was going to be a deal.

An unknown factor troubling me was: Could this Mr. Dean be persuaded to sell the holiday camp site from which he had been trading since before the war? Perhaps he was keen to get back into business. It did not look, though, as if he had made a start on repairs.

Every man is supposed to have his price, even though I was not immediately familiar with Walpole's famous quotation, but, with a fully utilised overdraft limit of £500 at the Corn Street branch of

Barclays Bank in Bristol, I was hardly in a position to be too generous. What should I be offering? I had no idea of land values but the site was exactly what I had been hoping to find during my searches along the Somerset coastline.

All manner of thoughts were racing through my mind when twelve year old Valerie Dean answered my knock on the front door and she called out to her mother that a gentleman was asking to see her daddy. There was something of an anticlimax as far as my anxious expectancy was concerned. Leslie Dean was not at home. He was at the other of his holiday camp sites at Osmington Bay, near Weymouth in Dorset, where he was making preparations for a re-opening.

I was a little concerned at this news. Would he be re-opening the site I was after? Mrs Audrey Dean reassured me by saying that she felt that her husband could well be interested in selling the Brean Sands property. It was arranged that I would return at the weekend, by which time Leslie would be back from Dorset.

He would then be in a position to arrange a conducted tour of the site so that I could gain a better impression of the condition of the buildings. She said that her husband would also be able to provide details of the claim which had been submitted to the appropriate ministerial department in connection with the dilapidations.

Within the next few days a price of £23,000 was agreed, but this was to be for control of all the shares in the company which owned the site, not for the purchase of the actual property. On this basis the new owner would have the benefit of any monies received from the government by way of compensation for the damaged buildings. This was the sort of deal that I liked to put together and I felt that my mentor from pre-war days in the City, Martin Coles Harman, would have been proud of me.

My former employer was very much on my mind when I started my business, because I now had to find the money for the deal.

I had arranged to pay this significant sum of money for what amounted to no more than eight acres of land with about 100 wrecked and derelict buildings, including the dining hall, kitchen and ancillary offices. Yet I was absolutely convinced that I was about to enter a growth industry with enormous opportunities for expansion.

My experience in the City had led me to believe that investment capital was always available for really worthwhile propositions and I was determined that my newly purchased company would not only be successful but the shares would be quoted on the London Stock Exchange, thus realising one of my long-held ambitions.

I decided to set up a syndicate of personal investors to subscribe for 50% of the capital in the company and lost no time in making contact with some of my pre-war City connections, including Harman and Reginald Binns, both of whom agreed to give their support to my new venture. Another investor was Bill Smith, who was in the meat trade, and he was joined by a plastic button manufacturer called Alex Bernstein. I also persuaded Rex Randall, one of my bookmaker friends, to make an investment. Together this group of individual investors put up the sum of £12,500 for 50% of my new holiday camp company.

This cash-raising exercise took place before Business Plans became a vogue term, yet I managed to persuade everyone that this was a proposition that was well worth a modest investment.

Looking back, they could well have thought that I was suffering from some form of Orcadian madness, but, no doubt recalling the ability I had demonstrated in my pre-war days, they had the necessary confidence to back my foresight. The lure of a prospective quoted investment was an important consideration after a period of financial dormancy as far as the capital markets were concerned.

They were looking to me to produce an attractive return on their investment. They were not to be disappointed.

I quickly sold out my interest in the Bedminster business to my partner and this raised a somewhat gratifying amount of £2,000. My bank manager, Mr. Collins at Barclays Bank in Bristol, was not only impressed by my infectious optimism but was also prepared to admit to taking a liking to my blue eyes. He agreed that the bank would lend the sum of £10,500. For internal technical reasons associated with individual discretionary powers in lending money without reference to Head Office, this was initially made available by contributions from other branches in Somerset, including Highbridge and Burnham-on-Sea.

This enabled me to acquire control of the remaining 50% of the shares in Brean Sands Holiday Camp Limited. I changed the name to Pontin's Holiday Camps Limited . . . I had plans for future expansion.

After a year or so the bank's financial support was consolidated in one account at the Corn Street branch. Mr Collins did not know it at the time, but he had acquired a first-class customer for his employers and he did well in his future career with Barclays. He eventually became a local director and joined the board as a non-executive director of Pontin's on his retirement from the bank.

The company now had an authorised and issued capital of £5,000 represented by 5,000 shares, each with a par value of £1. As Leslie Dean's asking price was almost £5 for each share, the new owners had already awarded the shares a premium rating even though the underlying asset, the debutante to the post-war holiday camp industry, was still a shambles, let alone open for business.

I was appointed Chairman and Managing Director and each shareholder was invited to become a director of the company, although Harman and one of the others were to be represented by nominees. The Harman nominee, Dickie Doyle, was to stay on the board for many vital years

Leslie Dean also joined the board so that everyone could have the benefit of his experience. He was, after all, the only person among us who had the faintest idea of how a holiday camp should be operated. I am a quick learner, though, and soon proved that I had an inherent instinct for what the public wanted.

Urgent repairs were needed at Brean Sands and a workforce was recruited from the accommodation camp in Bedminster. Because of their five-day working week, the men were available on Saturday mornings, so I hired three coaches to bring them over. Renovations took place over three consecutive weekends in June.

The construction workers received cash and as many sandwiches as they could eat. There was also a ready supply of the local ale, which seemed to help get the task completed in good time for the start of the season in mid-July.

I had been busy, meanwhile, in acquiring furniture, bed linen, pots and pans and cutlery from the war-surplus sales being held by the Ministry of Works. These items were not exactly of the highest quality but I was working on the basis that people would be prepared to make allowances after the privations of the war years.

Attracting the first customers proved to be no trouble at all. Just one advertisement was placed in the *Sunday Express* and thousands of enquiries poured into the hastily furnished office at Brean Sands.

Members of staff were recruited locally, but the lack of experience was becoming only too obvious. After two weeks of rather disorganised operations I decided that I needed some help from my family. My brother Len had gone back to his old job with Tote Investors after he was demobilised from the army, but, at the age of 27, he was soon looking for a position which offered better prospects.

When my 'rescue' telephone call came he did not hesitate in shooting down to Weston-super-Mare railway station, where I picked him up in the car at eight o'clock in the evening and we drove to Brean Sands. He still remembers finding the camp absolutely bursting with people and activity but nothing but chaos as far as the administrative side of the business was concerned. This was why he was there and he had no time to enjoy the local scenery.

We worked together on the mass of paperwork which had accumulated, but at midnight Len and I took off to the dining room, which doubled as a dance hall. This was so we could assist in the preparation of the sausage sandwiches and hot coffee which were offered to the guests at the end of each evening's entertainment.

This little routine became a firm favourite with the holidaymakers and resulted in a welcome boost to the cash takings. It also illustrated my willingness to turn my hand to any task which brought me into regular and direct contact with my guests. This would be an important feature of my future policy.

Thousands of my most loyal customers have always appreciated this accessibility and of my readiness to have a drink and a chat whenever they came across me during the course of my regular visits to each of my future sites. If I had any secret when establishing this type of relationship with my guests it must be what I can only describe as an instinctive perception of what my clients were seeking on their annual holidays.

In *Goodnight Campers*, sub-titled 'The History of the British Holiday Camp' by Colin Ward and Dennis Hardy and published by Mansell in 1986, it is stated that holiday camps were popular because they met aspirations which involved 'the popular utopia, food and drink are plentiful, there is constant entertainment, and chores are done by others'.

Looking back over what we were all seeking to achieve in those days, I can only say that we must have got it just about right. People kept coming back for more, year after year. There were, however, certain social geographic reasons for the success of businesses such as mine and I will refer to these later.

Catching on quickly to this camp business, I realised before too many weeks had passed that established sites were a far better basis for expansion than developing derelict properties.

Leslie Dean's other holiday camp at Osmington Bay was, therefore, soon to become the subject of some hurried negotiations. Osmington, which had a fine coastal position overlooking Portland and Weymouth Bay, was not too far away from Brean Sands, so management and supervision were not likely to be problems.

Although the camp had been requisitioned during the war the chalets and other buildings were in far better condition than those at Brean, so Leslie Dean and his partner George Harrison were determined to extract a much more favourable price than they had achieved for their other property. The camp had been newly decorated and was fully furnished. Their opening figure was £50,000, but, after a short period of bargaining, I managed to obtain an agreement to sell at the price of £46,000.

Osmington, with 220 beds, opened just a few weeks after Brean Sands, which had 198, and both holiday camps worked to virtually maximum capacity.

As early as the second year of operations I became aware that the growth of the business required sound administrative control, so I persuaded Ann Miller to accept a position with the company. She was then 31 years of age and had continued her career with the Ministry of Food.

She had been posted to Winchester, where she found life to be very monotonous and uninteresting.

Our relationship was such that I had kept in very close contact. Ann became very enthusiastic about the prospect of joining the rapidly expanding group at a time when bookings were coming in at ever increasing levels.

She was commercially qualified, having graduated from Edinburgh University just before the war, and she shared my enthusiasm for the aquisition of more holiday centres to satisfy the demand for family holidays.

Her first duties were to travel around the sites to supervise the complicated rationing procedures still in force. She set up home in Berrow, just a short distance from Brean Sands.

I have no hesitation in saying that without Ann Miller my business would never have achieved such an outstanding trading performance. I have confirmed this publicly on several occasions and it gives me great pleasure to do so again.

It eventually became clear that Osmington would be an ideal headquarters for the business. Ann's organisational capabilities and her talents as a sound adminstrator were soon very much in evidence with Osmington Bay becoming her prime responsibility as an operational holiday centre and as the group's head office.

She was appointed to the local board and, although Osmington was being advertised as a camp 'under the owner's personal supervision', it was Ann who was responsible until Colonel Walter Rowley took over in 1961.

During the 1946 holiday season the off-peak, all-inclusive tariff at both the Brean and Osmington holiday venues did not exceed £7 per week. I was determined to live up to my well-publicised slogan of providing value for money. My pricing policy was based upon a belief that a holiday at one of my camps should not cost more than a week's wages for an average working man, a formula which still tends to hold good even in the 1990s.

At the end of that first season, though I increased the peak weekly tariff to £10, Captain Harry Warner, one of my closest competitors and a pre-war pioneer in holiday camps, told me that I would ruin the business by charging what I could only describe as a worthwhile premium for the peak periods of school holidays. I was quick to reply that holidays would never again be so cheap.

This proved to be correct and others were soon to be adopting my policy, although I still consider that we gave the best value for money.

We decided to celebrate our first Christmas in a big way after our hectic, but profitable inaugural summer season of 1946, when we had already earned a reputation for being a close-knit, family-operated company. We found ourselves responding positively to suggestions that we should open Osmington Bay for what could be described as a 'Christmas reunion' for some of the friends we made during the summer months.

We had been breeding ducks, chickens, geese and turkeys at Brean Sands so these were slaughtered and transported down to Osmington in an old military ambulance which we christened the Blood Wagon. This vehicle was extremely prone to regular breakdowns so I took the precaution of bringing up the rear in my own car.

It should be remembered that these were times of rationing: even bread was rationed and in short supply and meat, in any shape or form, was available in only minute, strictly controlled, portions.

My aim was to create goodwill for the 1947 season, bearing in mind I already had plans for expansion, with Bracklesham Bay within my sights.

Between three and four hundred bookings were taken for Christmas at Osmington Bay, but three days before the guests were due to arrive large areas of the country were in the grip of harsh winter weather. Osmington was snowed in.

The approach road is narrow and winding to a site perched on the top of a cliff. Not the best of conditions when the ground is covered by six inches of snow. Miraculously, there was a thaw and everyone reached us in time for Christmas Eve. Very few people had a car in those days so we arranged to meet the various trains with coach transport.

The weather improved to such an extent that we enjoyed Springlike conditions. We were determined to give everyone a Christmas they would never forget. We had log fires, seven and eight course meals and food the like of which had not been seen since before the war.

I cannot recall how we entertained everyone, but I do remember that there was a marvellously unique atmosphere which couldn't possibly be re-captured. The circumstances were perfect . . . we had a lot to celebrate and much to look forward to, though the risk of bad weather was very much on my thoughts.

No attempt was made to repeat the exercise on a large scale throughout the group until the 1970's, by which time all of our facilities were vastly improved and communications generally were far more reliable.

My sister, Elsie did, however, experiment with a Christmas opening at Barton Hall in 1958, but this was considered to be a failure because she felt that the premises were inadequate. She resumed operations when the new wing had been built and she was provided with a ballroom.

From then on she had many years of successful Christmas festivities. There was always a waiting-list and she was known to boast: 'You can't get into a Barton Hall Christmas unless someone's died!'

Her standards were such that the male staff always wore dinner jackets, with the Pontin's girls in evening dress. Guests also rose to the occasion with the majority dressing for dinner in the traditional way.

By today's standards, the accommodation offered at Pontin's holiday centres during the 1946 season was very primitive. Very few, if any, of the wooden huts had cold water plumbing. Lavatories, baths and showers were available in purpose-built blocks, but even when some of the chalets were provided with wash basins for the 1947 season, hot water was obtainable only from a steam pipe usually located on the side wall of the kitchen. Guests were invited to take their water jugs to this facility if they wished to wash and shave in the comfort of their own accommodation.

Food continued to be rationed until 1954, but my wartime experience was to serve me well when I consulted my chefs about the daily menus. We provided three meals each day: breakfast, lunch and dinner, all served by waitresses in the main dining room.

Most of my customers were happy, and I felt that we really were giving value for money in those days of post-war shortages.

*My father Frederick.*

*My mother Elizabeth.*

*An early family group with mother. Stanley (left), Harry and my 'angelic' self!*

My second camp, and some of my first happy campers, at Osmington Bay, Dorset, looking towards Portland Harbour.

THE BAR

A TUCK CARD

CHILDREN'S PLAYGROUND

PONTIN'S SAND BAY
HOLIDAY CAMP

THE DINING HALL

THE BALLROOM

SB 44

...AY CAMP

THE FRONT LAWN

*One of our first 'wish-you-were-here' postcards from Sand Bay, near Weston-super-Mare in the Forties.*

*We could afford uniforms for staff at Osmington Bay by the Fifties. Ann Miller is on my right.*

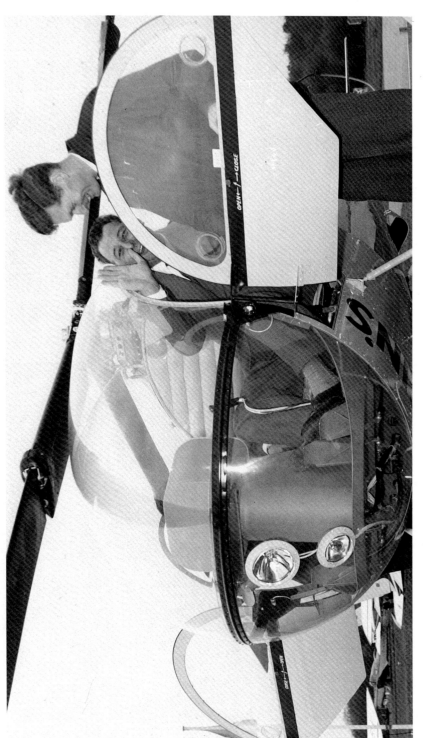

*My whirlybird days when 'The Guv'nor' would drop in by personal helicopter.*

*A night out with my daughter Patricia.*

*Telling Max Bygraves a story for a change!*

*Holiday camp 'Kings' together. (l to r) Sir Billy Butlin, Alan Warner, myself and Bill Warner.*

# IS THIS GILES'S MASTERPIECE?

More people than he's ever put in a drawing before

COME TO PONTINS

*Fame at last. Sunday Express cartoonist Giles pays tribute with a bumper-sized drawing.*

## HAVE YOU A MAGNIFYING GLASS?

*Just take a look, for instance, at the spiv outside the billiards saloon*

*Chapter Six*

# TYCOON AT LAST

THE TIME had now come for me to realise my ambition of launching a publicly quoted company on the London Stock Exchange. I consulted Martin Coles Harman, who, after referring the matter to Barclays Bank, recommended a provincial stockbroker to handle the issue.

The name put forward was the Bristol firm of Laws & Co. There had been a long connection and close association with the main branch of Barclays Bank in that city. Thurlow Laws, the senior partner, was introduced to me and we travelled down to Brean Sands together.

In later years, when Thurlow and I reminisced on the early days, he made reference to my description of Brean Sands as a 'proud collection of dog kennels'. 'Kennels' which proved to be the foundation stone of a great empire.

Brean will always be my first love, but it was not until 1963 that the original huts were replaced by brick-built, self-contained chalets, each complete with kitchen, bathroom and television set.

Senior local director of Barclays in Bristol was the Hon, "Bill" Bathurst, who was soon to become infected with my undiminished confidence and enthusiasm. Barclays agreed to act as bankers to the issue, and it is an indication of my penchant for loyalty that they remain my bankers to the present day.

The company also needed auditors and reporting accountants. Leslie Dean and George Harrison introduced me to Percy Cansdale, whose firm, Cansdale & Co continued to act for the company until the time of the merger with Coral in 1979.

Laws & Co organised support for the issue in the City of London, Thurlow Laws having previously prepared a prospectus which made use of the earnings records of all quoted holiday camp companies. On the basis of their profit-earnings ratios the prospects for Brean Sands and Osmington looked attractive. The issue was poised for success.

My founder shareholders decided to raise the money to buy the Osmington camp by issuing at par value 45,000 new shares of £1 each, all of which were fully subscribed by the original members. These shares were placed by Laws & Co., and I derived a great deal of satisfaction at the confidence being shown in my new venture by the investment community.

On the other hand, I recall that a partner in Clifford Turner, a well established firm of solicitors with an excellent reputation in the City of London, exclaiming, after listening to my plans to take the company to Stock Exchange: 'Well Pontin, we will do our best to keep you out of prison'. I was not put off by this cynical response to the – admittedly ambitious – proposals of a prospective client.

Prior to the placing, the whole of the issued capital of 50,000 £1 fully-paid shares in Pontin's Holiday Camps Limited was divided into 500,000 shares, each with a par value of two shillings (10p). The shares were soon starting to be traded quite actively at a price of seven shillings and sixpence (37$\frac{1}{2}$p), compared with the placing prices, which ranged from three shillings and sixpence (17$\frac{1}{2}$p) to six shillings and sixpence (32$\frac{1}{2}$p), providing some of the new body of shareholders with some useful profits.

The company satisfied all the requirements necessary to obtain a quotation in the days immediately after the 1939-45 war, and the upward movements in the share price soon brought Pontin's some respectful attention.

I was more than happy to reward Thurlow Laws with a seat on the board of the newly-quoted public company and he continued to be my firm friend and loyal supporter up until the time of his death in the 1980's.

Thurlow's own autobiography made generous references to his connections with me. He described the Pontin's issue as the most memorable of his long career, in that it gave him the most pleasure and satisfaction. Laws & Co, is still very much in existence as much-respected provincial stockbrokers, with Thurlow's son, Mr Charles Laws, as the Senior Partner.

Early in 1947 the shareholders were delighted to learn from their proud Chairman and Managing Director that the trading profit for the first operational season was some £17,000, thus producing an excellent return on their newly invested capital. It was at this time that a grateful board of directors demonstrated their appreciation by awarding me a service contract, which, if it was intended to work as an incentive, certainly produced the required results.

The contract provided for me, as their Chairman and Managing Director to receive, in addition to a basic annual salary of £2,000, 5% of the company's net profit before tax at the end of every year in which I held this position until I reached the age of 70. In 1976, the year in which I celebrated three score years and ten, and 30 years after taking over Brean Sands, the pre-tax profits of the group were £4,764,000, which would have resulted in my earning over a quarter of a million pounds – making me the highest paid company director in the United Kingdom.

In the event, and as was the case in previous years, I felt that the company could put the money to better use than me, especially as the Government would help themselves to a large slice of it in the form of their penal rates of personal taxation. I therefore waived my rights to the full entitlement and was content with my basic salary, which by then had been increased to some £50,000 per annum.

These facts are probably not well known, despite being publicised with the annual results. Although I had no hesitation in not taking advantage of the terms of the contract, I cannot tell you how much satisfaction it gave me at the time when my directors were prepared to be so generous.

The presence of this contract in my favour was a signifcant deterrent as far as unwelcome predators were concerned. In the 1960s and early Seventies any takeover bid for Pontin's would have had to take into account such a hefty prior charge on the company's annual profits, and compensation for termination of the contract would have undoubtedly cost the purchaser a great deal of money. It was not until I had passed my seventieth birthday that this inhibiting factor was removed.

Although I have always enjoyed the personal rewards and nationwide recognition which my charitable and business activities have earned over the years, I am quite sure that a close inspection of the underlying circumstances will reveal the tremendous benefits which have accrued for the benefit of the company's many shareholders.

At one time, these were many tens of thousands, but towards the end of its existence as an independent company the numbers were considerably reduced to a figure of less than 30,000.

Financial institutions, which have an enormous flow of cash that has to be invested on a basis of creating a well-balanced portfolio, have taken much greater control of public companies, and not always on a basis which has been acceptable to the minority shareholders.

My personal shareholders were always a great source of joy. Large numbers took the trouble to attend our annual general meetings, which were usually held on or around the date of my birthday, when I had much pleasure in giving an off-the-cuff and purely informal report on the company's activities, once the formal proceedings had come to an end. This always seemed to be appreciated, for it created a form of family atmosphere at what would normally be rather stuffy affairs.

During 1947, faced with applications for more holidays than we could supply from our two camps, I set about the acquisition of four additional sites: Sand Bay, Weston-super-Mare; Buckleigh Place, Westward Ho! near Bideford, North Devon; the South Devon Holiday Camp just outside of Paignton at King's Ash Hill; and Bracklesham Bay, Sussex.

With my empire growing I was thoroughly enjoying myself and certainly making up for lost time in my efforts to make my fortune.

I am not a modest man by any means and I have always liked to think that I became a firm favourite with my guests, so I lost no opportunity in publicising my new business. Leisure was fun not just for the holidaymakers but also for the management.

I was given a free rein by my shareholders and board of directors. It was my business and I was able to run it my own way without any hint of intereference. To all intents and purposes I was the company and it soon showed, not only as far as my staff and guests were concerned but also at meetings of the National Federation of Permanent Holiday Camps, where other members soon became aware that there was now a new force on the scene. The industry would have to change for the better, whether they liked it or not.

It proved to be very hard work for a comparatively short season, but success can become an addiction. I was only too willing to succumb to the temptations associated with prosperity and I am the first to admit that I have remained an addict to this very day.

Twelve months of travelling and skilful negotiating had added a total of 910 extra beds which, together with Osmington and Brean Sands, now gave me control of over 1,300 units of holiday accommodation at six separate locations.

Compare this with Billy Butlin's ownership of Pwllheli Holiday Camp, which as far back as 1948 could accommodate a total of no less than 5,500 holidaymakers in one location, and the differences in our business philosophy will be readily appreciated.

I took the view that to have the task of filling literally thousands of beds on one site for every week of the holiday season, as well as to entertain and feed all of the guests with food rationing still very much in evidence, were managerial problems of such insurmountable proportions that I felt that I had no wish to be in that particular market.

Although Butlin's was to prove to be a successful company, the business never enjoyed the cachet of Pontin's more manageable centres. This was the key to my considerable personal success and the rapid growth in popularity of every one of my company's holiday centres. Pricing policy did, however, have its part to play.

In 1948 Billy Butlin was offering a total of 21,500 beds in five separate locations. These were large sites, some of over 300 acres, and more than half of the chalets had hot as well as cold water facilities. Organised entertainment was on a large scale, though his guests were being asked to pay at twice the rate charged at Pontin's camps.

I was at the other end of the market, yet Billy Butlin was worried enough to take the trouble to see what his newest competitor was up to. With one of his colleagues, Basil Brown, he just happened to be photographed taking a drink in the bar at Brean Sands.

Jack Sullivan was the camp photographer at the time and, some years later, he recognised Billy's face and brought the matter to my attention. I was quick to take advantage of this somewhat unauthorised intrusion by a close rival so I published the picture in our annual brochure – with a caption drawing attention to where Billy Butlin spent some of his leisure time, using the slogan 'All the best people came to Pontin's'.

It was very much a tongue-in-cheek type of reaction, but an excellent example of my aggressive marketing techniques. Billy was none too pleased, but he did not take it too seriously once he got over his initial irritation at my effrontery.

Billy Butlin once offered me control of his company. He thought of taking less interest in his holiday empire because of the penal personal taxes he was having to pay. In the event his overtures, and my qualified response, were not to be tested. Billy was not able to secure the agreement of his board, who seemed to be very much against any thought of Pontin's being in control of their sites.

With a good team and an ever-increasing demand for our brand of holidays, I was determined to add to the assets of Pontin's Camps Limited, but felt that I could not expect the board to back my judgement until such time as the new acquisitions were seen to be profitable.

The audited accounts of each prospective purchase provided little justification for optimism in terms of future success, though I was certain that I had the right formula and that a period under my management could transform a previously indifferent trading performance. I decided to shoulder the risks and embarked upon a policy of using my own as well as the bank's money to finance the expansion programme.

Leslie Dean and, on occasions, George Harrison became my partners in these operations. When we sold the new businesses to Pontin's, usually at the end of the first year of trading, it was at cost price plus the equivalent of the first year's profits. These were paper transactions with each partner taking shares in Pontin's in exchange for the new sites. In this way I was able to build up my shareholding in Pontin's and at the same time consolidate and increase my influence within the company.

The quality and quantity of food were always important factors. For the 1948 season I hit upon the idea of opening a small unit camp in Trabolgan, County Cork in the Irish Republic, where there were no rationing restrictions. I acquired with some Irish partners control of a 120 acre private estate where we were able to accommodate 200 guests in brick-built chalets. All had hot and cold running water. There was additional room for 60 visitors in the main house, previously the home of Lord Fermoy.

This holiday centre proved to be very popular for only a year or so, because its popularity amongst the British took a turn for the worse when food rationing restrictions were eased and an overseas travel allowance became available to a population which had been starved of overseas travel.

The Irish never seemed to take to the holiday camp concept, but money was not too plentiful in Eire in those days anyway. It was to be many years before this Irish venture ceased to be a problem, though there was some personal consolation as far as myself and founder shareholder and director Bill Smith were concerned.

I enjoyed regular visits to Eire, where I met the world-famous racehorse trainer, Vincent O'Brien, and his brothers at one of the very popular hunt balls in the main house at Trabolgan. They became firm friends, and as a result Bill Smith, always a staunch betting man, and I became the owners of several victorious National Hunt horses recommended by Vincent from his training stables in Mallow, Co. Cork.

This was to be the start of a very successful racing career for me, culminating in being the winning owner in the 1971 Grand National at Aintree, but more of that later.

Following the introduction of Trabolgan, making a total of seven holiday centres, Pontin's entered a period of consolidation that lasted through the early 1950s. Some of the surplus cash flow was utilised in upgrading the accommodation and other facilities.

I was constantly on the road, driving long distances in my newly acquired Bentley to make weekly visits to every holiday centre. This form of transport served me well for many years until 1963, when the company acquired an American Brantly helicopter for £10,000.

The new form of transport took away a lot of the strain and it made my visits much more spectacular. Large numbers of guests used to take photographs of the helicopter's approach and gather around the machine after it landed. Some people even asked for my autograph.

Photographic concessionaires would also do some good business because guests liked to have a record of being seen chatting to the Chairman who had just flown in.

I kept this two-seater helicopter for about three years and it proved to be a great time-saver.

We were always being hampered in the Fifties by building restrictions, the Government being more concerned in diverting resources elsewhere in what they described as the national interest. I always made a point of criticising this policy in my annual statements to shareholders to let them know that it was not my fault that improvements were being effected only on a long drawn out piecemeal basis.

As late as 1950, only Buckleigh Place and Trabolgan were advertised as having hot water available in the chalets. Other sites were brought into line as soon as it was possible to undertake the work.

There were some shortcomings, bearing in mind that we were dealing with pre-war structures, untrained staff and a general lack of expertise in mass-catering for people who wished to have nothing more than a jolly good time. There were elements of dissatisfaction and this was reflected in my postbag. I have kept a few letters dating back to 1948, during my third season, and they make interesting reading.

Water figures prominently. We advertised running water in the chalets – but some of my correspondents took exception to this being effected through the wooden roofs of their accommodation!

Our camps would often be near a caravan site and the increased number of summer visitors to the area was putting pressure on the water supplies. The water authorities had no money for investment so their answer was to reduce consumption by cutting off supplies or reducing the pressure during the course of each day. This had an unpopular effect on the lavatories as well as the showers and baths.

Food was always a problem. It was impossible to please everyone all of the time but we always did our best to give our guests plenty to eat, even if the quality did leave something to be desired. Those were the days of rationing, with some of the effects of war still being experienced.

Tinned Spam was not a popular item. One person complained that a fish course should 'always be followed by a substantial pudding', no doubt some form of hangover from his schooldays. Another felt campers were not getting enough cups of tea for the value of the ration coupons we collected from their books.

Another grumbler decided that cutting her soap coupon, but not laundering her sheets on more than one occasion during the course of her visit, was an inadequate service.

People also objected to paying for extras such as transport from the local railway station, an early morning cup of tea and afternoon tea with sandwiches and cakes – a service which was made available only in response to popular demand – so we decided to bring some of these features in on an 'all-inclusive' basis.

I tried to respond in a positive manner to all justifiable complaints and even went as far as to offer the compensation of half-price holidays in off-peak periods of the following season, but the letters still came, especially from 'professional bleaters' who could never be silenced. Being a member of the National Federation of Holiday Camps, I soon discovered that some names were known throughout the industry, so we devised an unoffical black-list.

By and large we experienced great loyalty and understanding from the vast majority of our guests. When restrictions were removed we set about improving all services and facilities. With this in mind, I explained to my shareholders that I was not in favour of increasing the dividend on an automatic basis every year because I would rather build up the company's cash reserves.

Whatever the nature of some of the complaints from our guests, we could not have been too unsuccessful in our efforts. The level of bookings continued to be very satisfactory and I was anxious to meet the increasing demand for what we had to offer.

By the 1960s the weekly dinner menus at Pontin's establishments tended to be based upon two roast beef, two roast chicken, one roast pork, one roast lamb and, on the last night of the week's stay, invariably roast turkey, with all the usual trimmings.

This type of traditional fare stood the test of time, and after the problems associated with rationing were behind us we got very few complaints.

*Chapter Seven*

# BOOM YEARS

WITH THE benefit of hindsight, it is clear that in seeking to expand my commercial empire I was not merely responding to demand but benefiting from a social revolution in the post-war years.

Clement Attlee's Labour administration of 1945 had enormous problems to contend with, but it has to be admitted that the policies of his government certainly assisted the working classes over and above other members in our capitalist society in the years that followed the Second World War.

When the Conservatives were returned in the early 1950s there was a continued improvement in living standards for working people. A phenomenon which led to Harold Macmillan's famous speech at Bedford in 1957, when he informed the British population that '. . . most people have never had it so good!'

This state of affairs was certainly to my benefit, because by far the majority of my guests were made up of British workers as opposed to the middle classes, who took a little longer to appreciate what we had to offer.

There was a significant redistribution of incomes in post-war Great Britain, and the people who benefited were my regular customers. I was not slow in recognising where some of this fresh spending-power was being directed. By 1958 wage earners were 27% better-off than they were in 1949 and even office workers were enjoying ten per cent more disposable income.

These were golden years as far as Britain's post-war living standards were concerned. Economists have written that these improvements were both absolute and relative, the advance of ordinary workers being truly remarkable.

It was not long before I was able to add to the number of holiday camps under my control. Three rights issues in 1954 and 1955 raised additional cash capital of £125,000 from my enthusiastic shareholders, who, in common with tens of thousands of Pontin's customers, felt that they were getting value for their money.

A beauty queen contest with prizes totalling 100 guineas was announced for both 1954 and 1955, and the reunion dance at London's Seymour Hall was billed as featuring Geraldo and his Orchestra.

The boom years of the Fifties attracted one particular investor on behalf of a major pension fund that is still benefiting today from this earlier shrewd decision.

In February 1959 I was persuaded to part with a number of Pontin's shares from my personal portfolio to the Imperial Tobacco Pension Fund. Their Investment Manager, George Ross Goobey, was introduced to me by Thurlow Laws, the Bristol stockbroker and a director of Pontin's from the early days.

My company had received the seal of approval from the Pension Fund Trustees on the recommendation of Ross Goobey and his immediate superior, P.V. Roberts, who was a director on the main board of Imperial Tobacco. These gentlemen had travelled down to South Devon with Thurlow Laws to see how we operated and – I have to say – we enjoyed a riotous evening together.

They went back convinced that me and my team were dedicated to our work and to the future prosperity of the holiday camp industry.

As a result of this meeting the pension fund acted as sub-underwriters to a succession of rights issues over several years by Pontin's Limited, the proceeds of which were utilised to finance certain acquisitions and camp improvements.

Unfortunately, and to the intense disappointment, not to say chagrin of Ross Goobey, the fund was never left with any shares. If it wanted to invest in the company it would have had to be done on the open market, where any large purchase would have driven up the value of the shares.

One evening at Murrays Club in the West End, where I had become an habitué, George took advantage of my good humour. Before we had consumed our last drinks he had secured my undertaking to sell his fund no less 100,000 of my *own* Pontin's shares at what was then the middle market price of three shillings and nine pence (18.75p) – an investment of £18,750.

During succeeding years there were various rights issues, capitalisation issues and scrip dividends, which, at the time of the later Coral takeover of Pontin's in 1978, left the fund with a total holding of one and a half million shares at an average price of two shillings and seven pence (12.91p) – a total of £193,650.

In exchange for this holding in Pontin's the fund received £368,000 in cash and 614,000 shares in Coral. In January 1981 Bass took over Coral and the Imperial Tobacco Pension Fund received 283,000 shares in Bass in return for the Coral holding.

By February 1991 Bass shares were quoted at £9.35 in a depressed market, but leaving the fund's original investment in Pontin's with a capital value of £2,646,050. This represents a profit of £2,452,400.

If any Imperial Tobacco pensioners find themselves reading this book, I trust that they will be truly thankful and pay tribute to the investment expertise of fund managers like Ross Goobey. He was a leading pioneer in persuading institutional investors to put a proportion of their portfolios into equity investments, as opposed to government securities.

Please bear in mind, however, how difficult the task was for George, having regard to the activities of people like Martin Coles Harman in the 1930s. Incidentally, George's son, Alistair, has also a fine reputation as an analyst in the City, and I often hear him acting as a stock market pundit on BBC Radio 4's *Today* programme.

I have been informed that the pension fund's original investment in Pontin's as represented above, is still intact, so I can only reflect on what additions there may have been to *my* personal wealth if I had decided not to sell the shares to dear old George. There is no question of any sour grapes, because over a period of many years he has been a loyal friend to both me and my company, and I shall always be grateful.

When building up a public limited company it is necessary to have friends who enjoy influence in high places, especially in the investment community, and I am pleased to say that after over 40 years of being associated with quoted companies I still have my loyal supporters and my name appears to be as sound as it ever was.

If I have one regret it is in connection with the outcome of the earlier efforts of Thurlow Laws to establish our name in the City.

The holiday camp industry had not really achieved any measure of respectability in the investment world in those early days. He wrote in his autobiography that he was not helped by the fact that, in his view quite wrongly, the Harman 'image' behind the company was unpopular in the City.

Although his interest was through his nominee, Dickie Doyle, the investment community is close-knit and Martin Coles Harman's spell in prison was not to be easily forgotten. He enjoyed my complete confidence, but he had nothing whatsoever to do with the running of Pontin's. That appeared to make little difference to attitudes generally, and Thurlow had to fight what he termed an uphill battle.

Eventually he hit upon the idea of seeking the sponsorship of a top London stockbroker and, after a sustained period of lobbying, he persuaded Simon & Coates to take a close look at me and my company. A luncheon was arranged and, according to Thurlow, I made a good job of selling myself.

I can only add that, as a matter of principle, I made a point of offering no apologies for my former employer because I did not consider that this was by any means appropriate.

My point must have been taken. Simon & Coates duly became our London brokers and, as a result, we had the backing of a first-class firm when we were making larger capital issues in the years that followed.

Needless to say, we did not let them or our shareholders have any cause for complaint as the company went from strength to strength. Both before and after the later Coral takeover my own relationship with the company became the subject of much comment in the financial Press... usually on the lines that I was the dominant personality, had been able to outpace my rivals, and that the management had consistently revolved around my personal commitment as Chairman and Managing Director.

It was agreed that the company was well-managed and that to all intents and purposes I had always nurtured the company as a child. Those who know me would not expect me to challenge these contentions, so I will allow them to remain on the record. You never know, one day I may have the need to use these quotations in my curriculum vitae!

As well as the money men, others were drawn to Pontin's in the Fifties. Growth in the business was soon to attract, also, other members of my family. My brother Harry, then aged 39, joined as manager at the newly acquired camp at Bracklesham Bay. He stayed there for a few years before assuming the role of a general factotum-cum-public relations officer for the burgeoning commercial enterprise.

My sister Elsie had been employed as an Assistant Food Executive Officer with the Ministry of Food in Bristol and her husband Bob Brown, had seen active service with the Irish Guards. I persuaded Bob to give up his 'pen pushing' (in his pre-war printing works) to take up the more challenging position as secretary at Brean Sands in time for the 1947 season.

Elsie did not join Bob when he went down to Somerset, but she did take mother and her niece down to see what a holiday camp looked like. I was amused when she admitted being horrified by the rudimentary accommodation and refused to sleep in one of the chalets. She was found a room in the bungalow occupied by the manager, Arthur James, who was Leslie Dean's brother-in-law.

Elsie recalls that the chalets measured about eight feet by six feet 'just like bathing huts', but she conceded that, as these small structures were being treated merely as places to sleep, it made good sense to keep the guests occupied throughout the day and spending money in the bars in the evenings.

My father had died during the war years. He had been employed as a Ministry of Works inspector and was based in Bristol to where the rest of the family moved from a temporary home in Brighton. Father fell, quite accidentally, from a train just outside a local railway station and was never to fully recover from his injuries.

The eventual cause of death was cancer of the lungs – he had been a heavy smoker – but we all felt that the accident was an important contributory factor to an early loss of the senior member of the family.

Our family still enjoys the use of many items of his fine furniture and I often recall the times when he stayed at stately homes and historic houses restoring important items of antique furniture.

It was not long before Elsie was persuaded to make use of her experience in food and catering and she and Bob moved down to the South Devon site to take over the respective positions of Catering Manager and Camp Manager.

They were to stay there for ten years before Elsie persuaded me to acquire, for the sum of £60,000, Barton Hall, Torquay. This acquisition was to prove to be of outstanding significance to the group. Elsie was not attracted by anything that was second-best, so she was determined to make Barton Hall a holiday centre with a difference.

She persuaded me to introduce a number of luxurious "Imperial" suites, which were fitted with carpets and named after the leading hotel in Torquay of the same name.

Barton Hall soon acquired a unique reputation for being the jewel in the crown of the Pontin's empire, even though in the early days it never had the benefit of the national publicity machine. It generated business by the guests returning year-after-year. More than 50% made their bookings for the next season before their day of departure. Press articles referred to it as 'the executives' holiday camp', where Jaguars and Bentleys parked alongside Minis and Cortinas,

Elsie and Bob established and maintained very high standards, putting execptionally good food at the top of their list of priorities, followed very closely by comfortable accommodation. Excellent sport and recreational facilities included the country's first artificial ski slope.

Lord Ted Willis, the writer, was a frequent visitor who appreciated the sparkling white linen, superb four and five course meals, wine waiter service and piano music during dinner. He continued with his regular holidays at Barton Hall, after his elevation to the Peerage and he even arranged for an episode of *Dixon of Dock Green*, his popular BBC TV series, to be filmed there.

We had the entire crew at Barton Hall, including the stars, who you may remember were Jack Warner, Arthur Rigby and Peter Byrne. PC Dixon and his family were portrayed as staying at a holiday camp and the producer gave me an Alfred Hitchcock type cameo role.

I was seen with my mother leaving the camp pub as PC Dixon and Sgt. Flint were making an entrance. All I can remember is that they kept shooting it over and over again. I would never make a film or TV star, though I did count the late Jack Warner among my friends. I succeeded him as president of the Thanet Dramatic Society in 1982 and donated holidays at my Farringford Hotel as prizes for their fund-raising activities.

Pontin's by now had sixteen holiday centres, in the Channel Islands, the South of England and Blackpool in the North.

My family took on ever-increasing responsibilities within the Pontin organisation, and Elsie, Len, Harry and Peter Hopper were rewarded with appointments to the board of the parent company.

Ann Miller also became a director and, although I did recruit senior executives – including some from the Butlin organisation – who also joined the main board, I always had the comfort of 'family' control.

This ensured support for any important and sometimes controversial decisions. These board appointments from the ranks of my family were, in general, replacing the majority of the original board of director/shareholders.

Bill Smith and Alex Bernstein retired from the scene in the 1950s but Rex Randall and Reggie Binns continued as directors until both died in 1962. Dickie Doyle retired in 1964, following many years of loyal support leaving me the sole remaining member of the original group of investors.

Thanks to Elsie and Bob, Barton Hall was a major contributor to the group's results, so, in accordance with my standard practice, I offered it to Pontin's Camps Limited. The deal was done against the issue of 300,000 ordinary shares, which further increased my stake in the public company.

This was one of the last deals I was to arrange on this basis because, after I had passed on Little Canada, my site on the Isle of Wight, on a similar basis, the major shareholders, particularly the institutions, severely criticised this type of transaction. They did this on the grounds that I was trading outside of the company's influence and then making a profit on the subsequent disposal.

I felt that their attitude was unfair and unjustified, bearing in mind that I had been taking the commercial risk, but I have to admit that I had not had to bear any losses.

I made two very significant site purchases in 1960 and 1961. I had always been keen to get into the Channel Islands, not just for low taxation but also because of the lower prices for alcoholic drinks which were more or less duty free . . . a great attraction to the vast majority of my traditional clients.

A holiday camp at Plemont Bay, Jersey was owned by a former showman, Stanley Parkin, who sought a purchase price of £500,000. I remember haggling with him because it was clear that the premises were in a very dilapidated condition and would require the 'Pontin's treatment' before we would get a worthwhile return on any investment.

We eventually agreed a figure of £375,000 after I heard that the Jersey Tourist Board were keen to have Pontin's on the island. The site was virtually re-built and before long we had a very attractive holiday centre which became very popular.

Our Channel Island guests also entered into the spirit of Jersey's Battle of Flowers, which is often described as one of the most joyous and colourful holiday spectacles anywhere in Europe. They always made a great contribution to the fun by manning our bloom-laden float in the procession through St Helier and along the Esplanade. I took the wheel of the vehicle on several occasions and not just for the publicity I can assure you.

Plemont Bay camp was owned and operated by a Jersey company, so when Billy Butlin retired to the island I was very pleased when he accepted my invitation to join the board of directors in a non-executive capacity. Other local directors were required including the previous owner Stanley Parkin.

As a footnote to the Jersey acquisition, Stanley Parkin demonstrated his loyalty to Pontin's by his continuing presence on the local board and he often flatters me by recounting the story of my purchase of his site. 'What I like about Fred Pontin is that if he shakes your hand the deal is done,' he is fond of saying.

I know what he means. When the lawyers and accountants get in on the act both purchaser and vendor can be thrown into confusion and what looks like a perfectly straightforward deal is seen to assume the proportions of a new constitution for world government!

The second important acquisition in this period was Blackpool, an operational unit with a coastal frontage half-a-mile in length. The entire share capital of Squires Gate Blackpool Holiday Camp Limited, was acquired in what I rate my best-ever deal.

It happened really by chance. I had flown from Blackpool to the Isle of Man to view one of the original holiday camp sites dating back to nearly the start of the century. The premises were dreadful so I flew back to Blackpool with the feeling that the day had been wasted. Someone mentioned the Squires Gate site in the Borough of Lytham St Annes and very close to the airport.

I had a brief look and made contact with owners, with whom I agreed the purchase of the company by an exchange of Pontin's shares, which were issued at a slight premium. Although I had to pull down most of the chalets, replacing them with modern units, as well as carry out a large-scale re-building programme, the purchase price of some £375,000 proved to be an absolute bargain.

I have always described the site as the best 'free house' in the country.

I was surprised, though, at the extent of the local opposition to my move into Blackpool. As late as March 1969 the *Sunday*

*Express* was telling its readers that Fred Pontin was upsetting the local landladies by describing his new site as "Pontin's, Blackpool". The property was, in fact, just 200 yards over the boundary in Lytham St Anne's and had previously been known as "Squires Gate Blackpool Holiday Camp".

This was enough for them to allege that the new name was an infringement of the Trade Descriptions Act. I was, of course, delighted by this response. It demonstrated, as was subsequently confirmed, that the centre was going to be much more successful under the new ownership and, as usual, the free publicity could only be welcomed.

The early Sixties saw another significant move northwards. I acquired a holiday camp at Middleton Tower, Morecambe from a Japanese gentleman who had built it from scratch, some say from a load of old packing cases which were once used for transporting gliders. I can believe it, given the condition of some of the chalets.

As this camp could accommodate 3,000 guests, it was necessary to recruit someone who had experience of such numbers. Butlin's was the obvious source and I managed to sign up Eric Bennett, who came with a sound recommendation from Tim Moorcroft, who had himself left Butlin's to join me only a few months previously.

Large unit camps required a different philosophy, but, although Eric Bennett, had the necessary experience, he will admit to having had quite a struggle during the course of the first year or so with Pontin's. He soon came to appreciate that my emphasis had always been on the quality of accommodation and catering, whereas the Butlin's accent was on entertainment.

What we did very successfully at Middleton Tower and at later large scale units was to combine the two. Within a few years Middleton Tower had been completely rebuilt.

It has a magnificent theatre, named the *SS Berengaria* after the ship which foundered off the Lancashire coast. It is a favourite venue for entertaining the many thousands of visitors attracted to Middleton Tower each year. The theatre building contains many fittings salvaged from the wrecked ship and boasts a stage which would be coveted by the manager of every provincial theatre in the land.

Our guests were now entertained for the very first time by a resident revue company, ably assisted by our own Blue Coats, who were also introduced to Pontin's in the early sixties. Billy Butlin had his Red Coats for entertainment purposes but our Blue Coats fulfilled other, and to my mind, more important functions.

They acted as hosts and hostesses: they organised games, sports and entertainments and generally went out of their way to ensure that everyone would feel completely at home on arrival at one of our centres.

Eric Bennett represented a new breed of manager for Pontin's and he undoubtedly joined us at a turning point in our progress towards big company status. He left Butlin's because he felt that their centres were getting too large to handle. When he left Butlin's Filey in 1960 there were 8,000 beds and such camps were operated by controllers, not managers. He soon appreciated that we were still a family company, but one which was going places.

He saw an opportunity for advancement and he took it, moving on to become General Manager at Blackpool, from where he retired in 1985.

We had our differences – Eric would always speak his mind – but our relationship was a lasting one, despite a period of suspension not long after he took over at Blackpool. We were having trouble with union penetration in the camps and we did not see eye to eye on a contentious matter, Eric taking the view that my attitude was positively Victorian as far as management-employee relationships were concerned.

All was soon well, however, and I am pleased to say that Eric is now in happy and active retirement in Kendal.

It is impossible to find enough space to mention all of the managerial staff with whom I have been privileged to work over all of these years. I trust, therefore, that my references to the work of Eric Bennett will serve as a tribute to everyone who had cause to suffer from the lashing of my tongue, then came to appreciate that my bark has indeed always been much worse than my bite.

I am told, though, that if Rotweilers had been about in my day I could have earned that nickname!

As time went by the tastes of our regular guests became more sophisticated, so we followed the latest trends. We graduated to self-service dining rooms by introducing the 'tray-and-away' systems, which were very cost-effective and brought in a wider choice of dishes, carousels for the display of puddings and salad bars.

Sister Elsie joined the main board in the late 1960s and she steered through this particular investment at six selected centres. The total capital cost was £250,000, a considerable sum of money in those days, but the payback was little more than a year as a result of savings on staff as well as food. There was much less wastage. I always said that the only people to lose out were the pig-swill contractors.

By the early 1960's all of my sites had been further modernised and extended in order to meet the growing demand for bigger, better and more comfortable facilities.

Self-catering was an important departure from the established pattern of the fully-inclusive nature of family holidays at around this time. This change in policy for some of the larger centres was not to be accomplished without controversial debates both within and outside the organisation.

In those days I talked about the new image 'Rent-a-Chalet' holidays, justifying the new approach by claiming that many of my guests were no longer prepared to be regimented to three meals a day taken only at set times. They wanted a change and a choice of their own.

We had entered the age when many families were becoming owners of a motor car for the very first time in their lives. They didn't want communal feeding and I was anxious to provide stiff competition for the caravan camps, which were growing in size and number. Providing organised entertainment in a self-catering environment might do the trick.

There are a number of alleged sources for the idea of converting selected camps to the self-catering concept.

Ann Miller claims to have conceived the original notion from her continual irritation at the patched hole in the roof of each of the accommodation huts which were occupied by servicemen during the war. Osmington Bay had 120 very nice timber chalets, but when the army heating stoves were removed a small sheet of asbestos was used to cover the holes in the ceilings.

After two or three years of coping with temperamental and unpredictable chefs, she had joked about putting the coke burning stoves back into the units – thus allowing the guests to prepare their own meals.

She now contends that this casual remark led to the policy of creating wholly self-catering holiday centres, which was looked upon in the early 60s as being quite a revolutionary concept for the industry.

An irony is that Osmington Bay still offers full board accommodation and has never catered for children, mainly because of the undulating terrain of the cliff top site.

Brother Len has his own version. He attributes the origin of the idea to his bank manager, who introduced Pontin's to a caravan and camping site at St Mary's Bay, Brixham, as a potential acquisition. Seasonal occupation of caravans and tents is, of course, synonymous with self-catering and the property was referred to me as a possible conversion into a holiday camp. The site was purchased and converted into a fully self-catering holiday centre.

I have always insisted self-catering holidays were my idea, because I was first in the field as far as the larger holiday centres were concerned. This latter point is an established fact, because Wick Ferry was the first site to be converted in this manner.

In the winter of 1961/62 I consulted my old friend Billy Butlin on the subject and his response was that working wives had no wish to work in the kitchen when they were away on their hard-earned annual holidays. My own view was that not all families wanted a cooked breakfast and could not afford a fully inclusive tariff which included a charge for something they had no wish to consume.

Some of my guests were making a habit of eating at restaurants outside of the holiday centres as a break from the normal routine. These were the type of people who would be attracted to self-catering holiday villages, which would continue to provide entertainment on an inclusive cost basis.

Whatever the source of the idea, there is now much hard evidence that Pontin's took the initiative in providing self-catering holiday centres. Others followed much later, but it was not before Bobby Butlin had taken over from his father that Butlin's followed the trend.

There was initial opposition from the National Federation of Permanent Holiday Camps, whose members considered that the entire concept of holiday camps would be lost for ever. They were misguided in this approach and I am certain that this important change of policy on my part led to the boom in holiday centres for the remainder of 1960's and the early part of the 1970's.

# Chapter Eight

# SPORTING LIFE

MY BOOMING business activities and my regular visits to Ireland once the Trabolgan camp had been opened in 1949 led to a keen interest in horseracing. Bill Smith, one of the original body of investors, was not only a close friend but also a keen gambler, especially at the races.

It was, however, a chance meeting with emergent trainer Vincent O'Brien and his two brothers at a hunt ball, traditionally held in the main house at Trabolgan, that led me to achieving the status of being an owner of a racehorse. O'Brien did not open his now world-famous training establishment on the 350 acre Ballydoyle estate until 1951. In those early days he had much more modest stables, comprising just eight boxes, in Mallow, Co. Cork.

He had taken out his first training licence in 1944, but it was 1948 before he started to achieve outstanding successes at Cheltenham with horses such as Cottage Rake, which won three successive Gold Cups, and Hatton's Grace, which won three successive Champion Hurdles. Vincent also trained three successive Grand National winners. He was still looking for customers in 1949, though, especially those who had the money to invest in horseracing, despite the austerity which was still in evidence after war.

It was much too early for me to be thinking about attracting publicity from my horseracing activities. That was to come much later when television cameras were a regular feature at racecourses all over Great Britain, Northern Ireland and the Irish Republic. In those early days I was probably lured by the excitement and camaraderie of the racing fraternity.

In addition to the novelty of having some surplus cash in my pocket, I had the advantage of having access to Bill Smith's considerable knowledge of the sport and its intricate terminology. As far as betting was concerned, I had never been drawn to gambling for its own sake, probably because of my pre-war activities as a bookmaker.

To have a direct interest in an *actual* runner was, however, quite a different matter. I was caught up by the stimulating atmosphere of racemeetings, not only in the Republic of Ireland but also at Cheltenham's National Hunt Festival, which always has the support of a strong Irish contingent.

My connection with Vincent O'Brien proved to be very profitable, and not just because of the results produced from the training of the horses. Together with Bill Smith I attended every meeting at which we had a runner. Our young trainer, whose influence and reputation were increasing at a rapid rate, invariably seemed able to guide us in the direction of successful horses. It would not be correct to say that the bookies were taken for a ride on every occasion, but there is no doubt that I enjoyed many celebrations with my horseracing friends in those early days.

Although I was not to know it at the time, my enthusiasm for the sport was to last over 20 years, during which time I achieved several spectacular successes including appearances in the winner's enclosure at Newbury and Aintree. These were during the course of the most important annual meetings at these famous venues.

Bill Smith was a partner in my early investments in the racing business. Vincent O'Brien bought two horses on our behalf. One was a complete failure, not even being placed, let alone winning, when it ran under our colours. Alberoni gave us our first taste of success, however, as well as some useful returns from the on-course bookmakers. It was at a Phoenix Park, Dublin meeting which saw this horse romp home from a big field as the 6-4 odds-on favourite.

Alberoni went on to win several other races over the next twelve months under its new colours, but Vincent O'Brien and Bill Smith anticipated my agreement to a sale of the horse at a worthwhile profit to someone who turned out to be Lord Derby's younger brother. As a new owner on the racing scene I had to accept the advice which had been given, but I was dismayed to learn at a later date that Alberoni not only continued to be successful but also won the Irish Grand National for its new owner.

There followed a few years of a routine, though very enjoyable, interest in horseracing. My relationship with Bill Smith became more distant when he went out to Kenya and retired from the board of the company, but this coincided with the time that the marketing advantages to be gained from horseracing became apparent as far as my continually expanding business empire was concerned.

I bought a horse called Gay Navaree after I had made it known that I wanted to own a winner of the Grand National Steeplechase at Aintree. Bill Marshall, the Cheltenham trainer, was instrumental in buying the horse on my behalf when he attended the Ascot sales.

This horse had twice been a finisher in the Grand National, but had then been taken out of training when the owner became mentally ill and was unable to attend to his affairs. The price was 2,700 guineas.

I was fortunate in being able to arrange for the name to be changed to Pontin-Go so we could cash in on the publicity generated by the horse's appearance at televised racemeetings, including the 1964 Grand National. Earlier in the year Pontin-Go had a fourth place at Kempton Park and was second in a race at Newcastle.

It was felt that it was a good prospect for the big race at Aintree, which had no less than four favourites, starting at 100-7. Pontin-Go was a rank outsider with odds in excess of 66-1.

Prior to the race there was a tragic accident near the Canal Turn. A light aircraft crashed killing five passengers, one of whom was Nancy Spain, the well-known TV personality, author and journalist, who was to have been a guest of Mrs Mirabel Topham, the owner of the Aintree racecourse.

The race did, however, take place and Pontin-Go ridden by P. Jones finished in fifth place after being second over the last jump.

This result gave enormous encouragement, not only to me but also to my management and staff – and my many clients who were starting to follow my racing activities with keen interest. I recall that the jockey was exhausted at the end of the race, but Pontin-Go was in fine condition, with ears still pricked and probably ready for a few more jumps.

Team Spirit's was a popular victory that year, having won by half-a-length in a very exciting finish, being fifth over the last jump. It would have been even more popular as far as I was concerned if an offer to sell me this particular horse had been put into effect just a little earlier. Before I could take advantage of what was the favourable price of 5,000 guineas the American owner disposed of a half interest and I could only dream about what might have been.

Pontin-Go made another appearance in the same race the following year but fell at the Canal Turn. I then took the horse out of training into a new career in Point to Point racing, ridden by the daughter of one of my employees.

Another of my Grand National prospects was foaled in France. The horse's name was identified with my latest venture in Europe. Go-Pontinental had a successful outing at the Yuletide Meeting in Liverpool on the fourth of December 1963, when it won the Santa Claus Juvenile Hurdle at 5-1. Bought on my behalf as well as trained by Bill Marshall, it had no less than 22 outings over the next two seasons, but only one further appearance in the winner's enclosure.

The horse continued to mature, though not in a particularly spectacular way until it won The Canterbury Handicap Steeplechase at Folkestone in October 1968, when it was ridden by Josh Gifford. Whatever the results, the publicity was always useful.

This horse qualified for the Grand National, having finished second by half-a-length in the Topham Stakes when it was again ridden by Josh Gifford, but on the big day it was brought down by a loose horse called Peace Town.

Go-Pontin, by the famous horse Pinza, was another candidate for the fulfilment of my racing ambitions. This horse carried high hopes as well as the name of the business, but after one or two unsuccessful outings, including a run in the company-sponsored Pontin Handicap Hurdle at Fontwell in 1963, it seemed clear that this was not going to be a world-beater. A buyer was found.

The horse continued to race under the name of Strapin, but with no success, thus justifying my decision. Once again, though, the company had the benefit of the short-term publicity.

I was not to know it at the time, but it was to be a few years before the ultimate success was to be achieved. This was not without a great deal of hard work and dogged perserverance in pursuit of my ultimate goal. When it happened it was during the same season. Nineteen-Seventy-One was a year I shall never forget, but before I recount the triumphant details it might be useful to explain my attitude to publicity and how I applied my theories to horseracing.

For obvious reasons, it can never be possible to arrange matters in a precise manner, otherwise I would be a multi-millionaire on the strength of my winnings from the bookies. My instructions to the jockeys were to endeavour to keep a horse in the first three or four places. On this basis the television or radio commentator would be constantly naming a horse associated with the title of the company or one of the sites.

There would be the drip, drip, drip of publicity directed at literally hundreds of thousands and, in the case of Eurovision coverage of the Grand National, millions of existing and potential clients of Pontin's.

Racehorses have always been an expensive luxury, but keeping them in training can always be justified if the resultant publicity results in substantial increases in annual turnover. Time and time again the results of market research demonstrated the worth of this form of activity. Who was I to complain if I was also enjoying the racing and all that went with the sport?

Unfortunately, I was not dealing with a bottomless pit as far as naming horses was concerned. The Jockey Club became aware of what was happening and they were not willing to see their sport exploited in this way. When George Wigg became chairman of the Horseracing Levy Board he took a firm line against my re-naming any further horses which came into my ownership.

I was to have the last laugh, as we shall see later, at the expense of the BBC television sports commentator and regular Grand National presenter, David Coleman.

But, for the moment, more about my most successful racehorses. Cala Mesquida was bought by Bill Marshall on a visit to France and I quickly named this latest acquisition after my very popular beach resort in Majorca. Trained by John Sutcliffe Senr, this proved to be a horse of real quality and I rather enjoyed becoming accustomed to success.

Its first season was 1969-1970. After a second place at Nottingham in October, Cala Mesquida succeeded in the Langley Handicap Hurdle at Windsor on 25 February 1970 at a price of 5-1. This was a memorable day for me, because not only did I win a substantial amount of money from a wager on Cala Mesquida, but at the same meeting I saw a horse called Specify brought home by Terry Biddlecombe as the 700th winner of his career in English racing.

The champagne had already been flowing and I was very much in the mood for a deal. Specify, which qualified for the Grand National by winning this race, was owned by Mr Paul Rackham, to whom I introduced myself.

It is said that some people make their own luck. On that particular day I pushed mine as far as it would go. I made it clear to Mr Rackham that I wanted to buy Specify, but he did not show any real interest in making a sale because he was also looking forward to having a runner in the big race at Aintree.

A few drinks and a happy atmosphere, however, soon produced some results. He named a figure of £15,000, which I felt was rather on the high side, my best offer having been £10,000. When I made what appeared to be an unsuccessful effort to split the difference at £12,500 I gained the impression that he wouldn't be averse to taking a flyer.

I persuaded him to agree to settle the price by the turn of a coin. If I won the price would be £12,500 but if he called correctly I would pay him his full asking figure of £15,000. I took a coin from my pocket and put it on the counter of the bar and invited him to make the call. He very kindly gave the honour to me and I called "heads" – Specify was mine for £12,500.

You have to agree that Sir W.S.Gilbert was close to the mark in his lyrics from *Iolanthe*:

*Faint heart never won fair lady!*
*Nothing venture, nothing win.*

My purchase of Specify attracted some very useful publicity because a lot of people were aware of my ambition to win the National. I recall John Lawrence – later to become Lord Oaksey – writing that I had paid far too much money for the prospect and he was not alone in his opinion. Again I was to have the last laugh.

Specify turned out to be quite a nervous horse, having broken a bone in its face when it fell in the 1968 Schweppes Gold Trophy. It had originally been raced hard on the flat as a two-year-old. When the horse became my property I entrusted him to John Sutcliffe to train alongside Cala Mesquida. Specify joined his stables at Ashtead, near Epsom, with instructions to prepare him for the 1970 Grand National.

This was not to be his year. Critics of my purchase felt that they had been vindicated. Although Specify was brought down at Beecher's Brook, he had performed well until this misfortune so I had no hesitation in entering him for next year's race. I had enormous faith in the horse and I tipped his victory to everyone who would listen, including what appeared to be my entire staff and a large proportion of my guests.

In the meantime, Cala Mesquida went on to win hurdle races at Folkestone and Nottingham at fairly short odds during the winter of 1969/70, but was disappointingly unplaced in the Benson & Hedges and Sovereign Handicap Hurdles at Sandown and Newbury respectively in December and January 1971.

Although I cannot be accused of being a pessimist, it was not a supremely confident Fred Pontin who travelled to Newbury on 13 February 1971 when Cala Mesquida was entered for the Schweppes Gold Trophy. This did not prevent me from tipping the horse, so there were many very happy people when he won a thrilling race on the last stride at a starting price of 33-1 from a field of 23 runners.

The rider was John Cook, who was booked to ride Specify in the 1971 Grand National. The national Press and racing enthusiasts then started talking about the prospect of a repeat success for the "Winning Trio" – John Sutcliffe, John Cook and Fred Pontin. They were not to be disappointed. We went on to produce a unique double.

I even had my own horse tipped to me by a couple I met in Miami, where I attended the Ali-Frazier fight in the company of the late Jack Solomons. These tipsters had obtained odds of 40-1 after getting their information from what they described as the horse's mouth. They had been given the word by John Sutcliffe, but were not aware that they were speaking to the owner. I had to wait to get back to England before placing my bet when the best odds I ever obtained were 33-1.

The night before the big day I had dinner with the BBC's David Coleman and his wife, Barbara. We knew each other from our respective charitable activities with the Variety Club of Great Britain. After a very convivial evening I had no hesitation in recommending that Specify should be backed to win next day's big race.

The future of the Grand National was then in some doubt. Mrs Topham, had been considering retirement as owner of Aintree. What should she do about a large area of freehold property which produced worthwhile returns on only one day of the year? The course was eventually bought by a property developer, Bill Davies, but mercifully the land has never been covered in houses and the most popular and most challenging steeplechase in the world is still a regular annual event.

The 1971 race was also distinguished by the fact that one of the jockeys was racing journalist John Lawrence, who was also a keen

amateur rider. In his report on the race he wrote that no Epsom
Derby could have produced a finer spectacle.

There was a desperate finish, with five horses together at the last
fence. Specify produced what Lawrence described as 'an extra gear
as miraculously, like the Red Sea, a gap opened near the rails
between Bongeeno and Black Secret'.

I quote again from his report: 'Specify went for the gap like a
terrier at a rat hole'. John Cook brought home what proved to be a
very popular winner as far as Pontin's staff and guests were
concerned.

This race was described as one of the most exciting Grand
Nationals on record and it is said that the entertainment provided
on that day did much to preserve the future of this great sporting
occasion. Someone wrote that after such 'a glorious race' could the
future of the Grand National ever be in doubt?

John Cook's performance in the race was described as a 'hands
and heels drive' and 'one of the coolest examples of jockeyship ever
seen'. I would not argue with these comments. It was very sad that
later that year John Cook suffered a broken leg, an injury which
was to finish his racing career. He later went out to Australia and
New Zealand where he became an assistant trainer.

I was unable to re-name Specify as 'Specify Pontins' due to
the efforts of George Wigg and the racing authorities, who
subsequently made it illegal to change a horse's name after it had
run as a two-year-old.

I made up for it when I was interviewed by David Coleman in
the winner's enclosure. Eurovision took the live broadcast that year
and, despite David's efforts to change the subject, I succeeded in
broadcasting the message to millions of viewers that the win by
Cala Mesquida in the Schweppes had 'provided the deposit for the
1971 Pontin's holiday', and now Specify's win had added 'the
balance of the cost, plus some spending money'.

I was overcome by exuberance of the occasion, but I did not
miss the chance to encourage the drip, drip, drip of publicity,
although on this particular occasion it was more of a deluge.
Perhaps David forgave me because he revealed later that he had
backed Specify to win the big race after my tip of the night before.

The publicity did not stop there. I entered Specify for the
same race in 1972 and the BBC obviously overlooked my
blatant plug because they featured John Sutcliffe, his wife
Claire, assistant trainer David Wilson, stable lad Ray McGhin

and yours truly, along with Specify, on the front cover of the *Radio Times*.

The inside story stated that I made no secret about why I was interested in racing, it being only for the publicity. They obviously felt that their viewers would be inspired to watch the race by publishing the picture and giving me such a write-up.

Incidentally, Specify's 1971 starting price was a generous 28-1, so a 'double' on Cala Mesquida and Specify would have produced incredible odds. What a pity I didn't think of it at the time. But I have already explained that I am not really a gambler!

This value of attendant publicity was particularly important because prize money in those days was very low, not much more than £15,000. By the time everyone had been paid there was not much available for lavish celebrations, yet the commercial benefits were very considerable. In modern times the winnings for the successful owner amount to some £100,000 and are much more significant.

The 1972 race was not to produce another miracle, even though I felt that he had an excellent chance. Specify, ridden by Bob Davies as a result of the injury to John Cook, ran a good race to finish sixth. This was before the days of Red Rum and until then no horse had ever won the race in two successive years.

My magnificent brown gelding was then thirteen years old so I retired it to the grounds of my hotel at Farringford on the Isle of Wight. This was once the home of Lord Tennyson. The poet's stables became the living quarters of Specify and his constant companion, an elderly donkey named Timber.

It seemed appropriate to have a retirement party for such a gallant racehorse so Specify was guest of honour at a celebration held at Farringford. Other guests were the training team, John Cook, who had by then announced his own retirement, Josh Gifford and Mirabel Topham.

When Specify eventually became too infirm he was put down by the local vet. Timber, by then 33 years of age, joined him on that same day in October 1982. I felt that it was only fitting that they should pass on to new pastures in each other's company.

After all this excitement, I started thinking in terms of winning a classic on the flat, so I bought a yearling. The horse was very well bred, but there were to be no more exhilarating successes. John Sutcliffe died from cancer in 1975 and I never looked around for another trainer.

I had achieved a great deal for myself and the company and I felt it best to rest on my laurels. John and Claire Sutcliffe were good friends and I used to enjoy driving down to the yard on Sunday mornings to have a yarn and see how the horses were getting on.

He had taken out a licence in 1965, just two years after his son, John Junr was born. Specify and Cala Mesquida were counted as two of his three principal accomplishments in the horseracing business. They were happy years. I am pleased that John found success with my horses.

An ironic footnote to this chapter is that in 1975 the Jockey Club amended their regulations so that owners could name their horses after a company's product or the company's name.

There are no hard feelings. I had got away with my little game – as did Sir Jack Cohen, founder of the Tesco supermarket chain. He had a horse called Tesco Boy, but he was not fortunate enough to emulate the achievements of his fellow Eastender, who had enjoyed a very good run for his money.

*Chapter Nine*

# THE GUV'NOR

ALTHOUGH I was a very dominant personality within the company, I have always been the first to appreciate that the foundations for success were built upon the 'family' image. Not just in terms of the involvement of my wife, daughter, son-in-law, brothers and sister, but by the long periods of service from many loyal employees.

It was not just the managers, but also catering, entertainments and maintenance staff. Perhaps this is best illustrated by a quote from Wally Riglar, who has been involved with the care and maintenance of Osmington Bay for over 40 years. He attributes the strength of Pontin's to the levels of hard work and dedication which were so much in evidence from all concerned in the early days.

'We all felt part of the team and one of the family,' he says. 'Mr Pontin always had time to discuss our problems and he and his family set an excellent example in terms of commitment to the success of the business.'

Wally's loyalty is very touching, especially as I know he commenced his employment with the company on wages as low as £6 a week. When he got married a few years later he was given a rise of £1.50 and he obtained a mortgage of £1,000 so he could purchase a bungalow at £1,850.

I recall that he was very nervous about taking on this commitment so I was happy to set his mind at rest by telling him: 'If you ever have a problem, come and see me'. He never did, but I know that this assurance was enough for him. The bungalow is now valued at £70,000 and Wally will get a good pension when he retires in the next year or so as a result of the scheme which I introduced to the company in the early 1970's.

When Corals took over Pontin's in 1978 for a short period the salary scales were brought into line with the main group and Wally Riglar was given a rise of no less than 28%, which must represent some form of indictment in respect of the levels of remuneration which were in evidence when I was running the company, particularly as some staff received even higher increases.

I have always been the first to appreciate that the foundations for success were built upon the 'family' image, not just in terms of the involvement of my wife, daughter, son-in-law, brothers and sister, but also as illustrated by the long periods of service from many loyal employees.

It was not just the managers but also catering, entertainments and maintenance staff. Pay increases were not always foremost in my mind when it came to looking after my staff.

I tended to offer some perks which I knew were very much appreciated. These were not large cash bonuses, which had an adverse effect on profitability, but were nonetheless just as attractive and created much goodwill.

The gift of a week's free holiday at one of our camps was a typical way of providing an extra reward for the more deserving members of the staff. When I was operating holidays abroad with Pontinental this created a new dimension, so large numbers of our employees took advantage of what appeared to be a very generous gesture on behalf of the management.

Perhaps it was, but it was also cost-effective. Spare seats on a charter aircraft were being taken, usually at the last minute, by members of the staff and their families. When they arrived at the resort they were making use of vacant accommodation – so the direct cost to the company was limited to food, some additional cleaning, and the laundering of bed linen.

There was, however, more than adequate compensation, because the bars and gift shops enjoyed increased takings. These arrangements, that kept everybody happy, did not really differ from the concessionary travel allowed to employees of airlines. These seats were usually made available on a strict stand-by basis, without significant cost to the company.

Talking of staff, I remember a Yorkshireman named Danny Horrigan. This was in the early Sixties and he claimed to be

Britain's happiest man, even though his summer job was to wash up 3,000 plates at Pontin's Riviera every day. Danny had a change each winter when he became a breakfast cook in a big commercial hotel.

He used to say, though: 'Give me the life at Pontin's every time. I enjoy my work and when it's finished there's fresh air, sun and friendliness to spare'. That's a good quote and serves to illustrate the phenomenon of staff dedication.

Another member of the staff, who started working for me in 1969 as a chalet porter and is now Operations Director of Holiday Club Pontin's, is Jeff Mallinson.

Jeff knows of many stories about me, some of which he says he would never disclose, but most of which I know to be apocryphal. He recently reminded me of an incident which took place in 1976, by which time his own dedication and potential had obviously been recognised because he had been promoted to General Manager of what in those days was our largest site, Prestatyn Sands Holiday Village.

Although he was the youngest executive ever to hold this post, Jeff had been told that his salary was to be regarded as provisional, pending the time when 'you have proved your worth', hopefully within a period of say two to three months. This was my way of keeping my managerial staff on their toes by promising rewards only when their performance provided the necessary justification.

Over the last few months of 1975 Jeff and his team ran several special events at Prestatyn, which were followed by a very successful Christmas operation and it seemed as though he felt that he had earned his increase in basic salary.

At the beginning of January 1976 the North Wales coastline was devastated by hurricane force winds which ripped the roofs from eleven chalet blocks and caused tidal waters to flood the holiday village and adjacent Grand Hotel twice during a period of 48 hours.

The following weekend they were hit again by similar storms, which destroyed five more roofs on the chalet blocks and again flooded the entire site. The damage ran into millions of pounds and insurance assessors were soon swarming all over the site.

Jeff led his team in the major task of reconstructing what remained of the holiday village and salvaging whatever was worth retaining for the coming season. I had kept in close touch with everything that had happened and I visited the site in early February to monitor progress for myself.

According to Jeff, I expressed much satisfaction at what had been achieved during what had been a comparatively short period of time and that everything appeared to be on course for the opening of the 1976 season. He must have been anxious to ensure that all was to my satisfaction. When he saw that I was pleased with what I had seen he tackled me about his rise just as I was about to climb into my car.

'I'm glad you are pleased with our achievements Mr Pontin. Can you now review my salary and give me my promised increase?' were Jeff's final remarks.

I turned round, faced him and roared: 'You have half-destroyed this holiday village, flooded it on at least three occasions and have the nerve to ask for a raise? No way, I say, no way!' If Jeff's memory serves him correctly I then gave a half-smile and drove away down the roads, now cleared of sand and silt and leaving behind a much-chastened General Manager.

There was a happy ending. Two months later he got his increase in salary, which is probably just as well – otherwise Holiday Club Pontin's would have had to look elsewhere for their Operations Manager.

Large numbers of purely seasonal workers were involved in my business. For example, in the 1970's Blackpool employed about 500 people, but the staff turnover in the course of a 26 week season could be as high as twice this figure. This would be exceptional, however, and mainly because of the competition from other employers in such a popular seaside resort.

Eddie Stamper, one of my longest-serving managers, who joined Osmington as a catering manager in 1968, prefers to maintain that the hard-core of his staff return year after year because they had become truly infected with the 'Pontin's disease', for which there is apparently no known cure.

He also talks of me attracting allegiances, but this is undoubtedly due to a way of life, not a personality. If anything, I am probably guilty of taking advantage of the job-dedication which has been shown over the years. If this is the case I cannot possibly have any regrets because the business is still there and it is thriving.

My site visits did not follow any set pattern, so the managers and staff were never given any advance warning from Head Office. If, however, there were two sites in fairly close proximity to each other the bush telegraph would work by means of a telephone call and the muttering of the password "coconuts".

Why this particular word should be used has never been revealed, and I can only assume that it had something to do with the sound of the clatter of horses hooves. I never did ride a horse but perhaps they felt that I was the Lone Ranger with Albert 'Maxie' Shirley as Tonto. Maxie was my chauffeur during the winter months over a number of years, having completed 'the knowledge' as a London taxi driver.

In the course of the season he was activities organiser at Osmington, where he was very well known, as he is today, for his Max Miller impersonations and entrepreneurial activities, ably assisted by Wally Riglar.

Maxie appeared on Gerald Scarfe's BBC2 television programme for the *40 Minutes* series. He was shown doing his act at the Hackney Empire. He is now aged 79 and often takes winter cruises with his wife Penny, still unable to resist appearing on talent nights with his Max Miller scripts to which he adds his own special jokes and songs.

I count Maxie as one of my old chums. He is a regular guest at my Farringford Hotel on the Isle of Wight, where I have a party of special friends every Christmas. He is our official Santa Claus and has also been known to respond to my requests to travel down and entertain the children – often at very short notice – if there is a period of prolonged bad weather during the summer months and there is a need for someone to cheer things up a bit.

When Walter Rowley was manager at Osmington Bay in the early Sixties and when Shortlake House, which is on the site, was my home base, I made a habit of visiting every other camp during the course of the week, but usually returned to Osmington in time for dinner on Friday evenings.

After my meal I would enjoy a short rest and then go on a tour of the bars before ending up in the ballroom, where, just before the usual rendering of *Auld Lang Syne,* Walter would make a point of introducing me to the guests. He liked to do this, but it wasn't really necessary. They had usually all had an opportunity to see me on my rounds, some had taken photographs, the odd one or two would even ask for my autograph and, if I they were feeling generous and had enjoyed a good week, would even buy me a drink.

Just as the band had played their last piece of music Walter would take the stage and announce my presence. The spotlights would switch from him to the balcony of what we knew as the 'Top Bar', where I would be standing, waving and smiling at everyone.

This became something of a ritual but Walter would not have stage-managed the operation if he did not feel that it was a worthwhile exercise. The response would not always be strictly complimentary. On one occasion, a guest nudged Walter and exclaimed: 'Look at him! Just like Emperor Nero up there, isn't he?'

I trust that he did not make the comparison in the literal sense because that particular historical figure had a reputation for cruelty and corruption and eventually committed suicide.

Regular site visits also kept me in close contact with my many guests, who appeared to appreciate that 'The Guv'nor' was prepared to stay in one of the chalets and eat the same meals at the same tables as themselves.

I enjoyed having drinks in the bar and I am told that there were many occasions when I demonstrated spontaneous generosity where it was felt that the situation warranted it.

This sounds to me that I was often in the habit of buying the odd round of drinks, especially if there had been grounds for complaint. Everything could not be expected to go right the whole of the time, but we did our best and people continued to return year after year, as they still do today.

All these efforts resulted in me becoming very well known to my management, staff and guests. Michael Austin, now Marketing Director at Holiday Club Pontin's, when interviewed by a journalist, told him: 'Mr Pontin is a hard man but fair, scrupulously fair'. I like to think that was an accurate description of how I was running the company.

I was also impressed when an early Sixties edition of *Investor's Chronicle* stated: 'Fred Pontin is a dedicated man with no interest outside his family and his business'. This was not strictly true, but it was the right thing to have written about you when you are anxious to impress investing institutions.

Tight control over expenditure was always being maintained. Whenever I visited our overseas sites it became routine procedure for the local managers to seek my personal approval for any improvements or replacements they wished to undertake.

We would go through each requirement, item by item, and the answers would come thick and fast – 'Yes, no, agreed, defer or never'. Before I left the premises the decisions would be committed to paper and I would take a copy back to Head Office, where Ann Miller would be responsible for taking any necessary action.

The system tended to be this informal, but it did work and everyone knew where they were.

I was not only looking for any readily apparent deficiencies, but also for signs of wastage. If I discovered something which might have been applicable to other camps I would issue a memorandum from the Chairman's office. I once decreed that 40 watt lightbulbs should be used in the winter months in places where it was not essential for a higher wattage.

You can imagine what I would have to say on the subject if a subsequent site visit revealed that my orders had not been put into effect. Repeated transgressions would be followed by a Chairman's Memorandum in vitriolic terminology with a copy circulated to every manager within the group.

Joe Rubido, one of my managerial staff at Torremolinos, recalls me putting my hands to my head and shouting 'My profits! My profits!' every time I heard a plate or a glass crash to the floor. This was all part of an act . . . I really wanted every member of the staff to know that any wastage was an anathema to me.

I never complained about the size of the portions of food or how much wine was consumed at the lunch and dinner tables, but I did hate waste. Everyone knew it. Joe said that my control was so tight that if I fell in the water I would never sink.

Despite Harry Warner once saying that Pontin, the newcomer, was ruining the business, I found that before too many years had passed I had gained a nationwide reputation for driving the product forward.

Recently this reputation was referred to by Mike Austin, who joined the Pontin organisation as one of my early proteges in the early 1960's. His present position is Marketing Director of Pontin's Limited, now a very profitable member of the Scottish & Newcastle group of companies.

He gives me much cause for satisfaction when he readily concedes that my knowledge of the business has been second to none, and that I played a leading part in raising standards at a time when there was widespread complacency in the holiday camp industry.

With customers returning year after year and most Pontin's centres fully booked, usually by early March, it needed a dedicated entrepreneur to continue to strive for higher standards in accommodation and facilities.

I used the regular meetings of the National Federation as a forum for the promotion of my ideas, such as introducing both indoor and outdoor heated swimming pools at some of the largest holiday centres.

I advocated the provision of more permanent forms of construction as far as units of accommodation were concerned . . . en-suite bathroom and toilet facilities . . . fitted kitchens in purpose-built chalets of bricks and mortar. All these improvements soon became the norm.

This was followed by the introduction of fitted carpets and even television sets. As the seasons became more extended I also made certain that heaters became a feature of the improved short-stay living quarters, which were now being offered to my increasing numbers of annual guests.

There was much scepticism about my determination to set new criteria in providing comfortable accommodation, not least from other members of the National Federation.

Mike Austin recalls that when I opened the newly acquired, and almost totally refurbished, holiday camp at Blackpool's Squires Gate, a local councillor remarked that Pontin's would be 'ruining the business in the area' by offering bathrooms and toilets in the new chalets.

He emphasised his point by saying that working people 'were content to have a good washdown when they left home and the same when they returned from their annual holiday'.

Although this ludicrous philosophy seems difficult to comprehend – even for the 1960s – his point that working-class holidaymakers didn't need such luxuries was really concealing the fact that the traditional seaside landladies would be forced to effect similar improvements if they were to continue competing for the lucrative trade in family holidays.

The fact that standards have steadily improved since those days is surely a tribute to my maxim that my company's reputation would be only as good as its worst accommodation.

My policies were vindicated by the group results for 1963, which set another record. Net profits before tax came out at £661,760, with £271,792 being distributed to grateful shareholders by way of an annual dividend.

The number of holiday centres in the United Kingdom increased to 18, following the acquisition of Broadreeds and Wick Ferry. Within ten years Pontin's had acquired six further sites, including Southport, Prestatyn, Camber Sands and Hemsby, Norfolk, which assisted in boosting annual profits to a shade under £2 million on a turnover of some £13 million.

Southport and Prestatyn were 'greenfield' sites, which involved the construction of entirely new complexes of buildings. The majority of the work was entrusted to a young man, Trevor Hemmings, who was eventually to join the board of my company. I had come a very long way from the short season at Brean Sands in 1946, but I wanted to remain a man who wished to be seen to be closely identified with his family business.

With the continuing growth of my holiday camp empire, Pontin's United Kingdom operations by the end of the 1977 season consisted of: 13 holiday camps with fully inclusive tariffs, 11 self-catering holiday centres and a chalet hotel in Jersey, Channel Islands. Overseas there were hotels and holiday clubs in Sardinia, Ibiza, Morocco, Spain and Majorca, where there was also a holiday village.

By this time group annual turnover had risen to approximately £39 million, of which over £10 million was from overseas activities. Pre-tax net profits were running at some £6,600,000 and shareholders were continuing to enjoy generous dividends.

Success in business inevitably leads to a thirst for achievement in other walks of life and over the years I was very fortunate to be able to indulge myself by participating in activities which not only gave me enormous pleasure, but also helped others less fortunate than myself.

I have never forgotten my roots, but at the same time have never had any inhibitions regarding an acceptance of a lifestyle which soon became second nature to the lad from the East End of London.

*Chapter Ten*

# COSTA DEL PONTIN'S

I MUST have been working at intense pressure, but I cannot say that I was unduly conscious of any strain. Despite the article in *Investor's Chronicle*, I did have outside interests.

I had my horseracing, the occasional night at a greyhound track, my activities with the Variety Club and I liked to enjoy a drink and a meal at well-known West End nightclubs.

All of these pursuits were an escape from the business, as was my membership of Jack Solomons' World Sporting Club. I had enjoyed boxing from my schooldays and loved to attend his many promotions. Pontin's often got involved with sponsorship at these events and part of the purse would often be a free holiday for two at a Pontinental holiday resort. The company got the publicity and I got the enjoyment.

Pontinental was yet another 'first' for yours truly, and what follows is a short introduction to the concept.

The impressive trading results were starting to include revenue from my incursion into what the travel writers then described as the sun-drenched beaches of Continental Europe under the banner of Pontinental Holidays.

I thought of this rather obvious name and this soon brought an exceptional degree of free publicity in the popular press. Holiday camps for foreigners? Has Fred Pontin gone mad? The journalists were, of course, missing the point.

I was intent upon exploiting cheap air travel by introducing my customers to the much more reliable weather conditions in the holiday resorts of southern Europe, not in selling holidays to the locals. A useful proportion of my Continental guests were to emanate, though, from these sources.

In the early Sixties my fellow directors did not share my enthusiasm for taking our successful formula for family holidays to the beaches of the Mediterranean. Yet the weather was far more reliable and the sun shone for much longer periods of time and over an extended summer season.

It was also clear that people liked getting sun-tanned to let everyone know that they had been away.

Ann Miller's first reaction was that she felt that the Continentals would not be attracted to what she felt was a peculiarly British-type of holiday. This was one of the very few occasions, though, when I did not accept her advice.

She now admits that she had really missed the point as far as my original plans were concerned, because it was my clear intention to offer our existing guests an even wider choice of holiday venue.

This was the time of cheap charter flights, so I calculated that I could offer two weeks in Sardinia or Majorca for approximately the same cost as a fortnight at Barton Hall.

I will not elaborate on the economics of the operation in any great detail, but the land was cheap, building costs, providing they were carefully controlled, were comparatively low and catering costs very competitive. I also planned to take advantage of some cheap loans from the Spanish Government, who were keen to promote tourism.

An important plus factor on the marketing side was, of course, cheap booze and plenty of it.

I am not going to pretend that there were no problems. The board felt that the United Kingdom business was producing very good returns and held the view that there seemed little justification for any speculative investment overseas.

I was not to be deterred, however, and I found support from not only loyal members of my staff, including Walter Rowley, my family and close friends, but also from City merchant bankers, M. Samuel and, at a later date, from American Express.

At one time I had Spanish partners, and their tastes proved to be extravagant. I was accustomed to watching every penny with my British operation, but exercising the same elements of control on overseas expenditure was far more difficult. There were also exchange control problems and the necessity to obtain permission from the Bank of England for all foreign currency transactions.

In retrospect, it must have been my legendary energy which carried me through. I enjoyed my overseas visits, however, and the thrill of finding locations, which in those days were often derelict tracts of land with no infrastructure. Yet they had the glorious advantage of being right on a beach with a clear blue sea just waiting for my first visitors.

Flights in unpressurised aircraft and landing on grass runways where there are now international airports also stand out in my memory.

As Pontin's original involvement was confined to merely a right to subscribe for up to £750,000 of share capital in Pontinental Limited at par out of the first £1,500,000 to be issued by that company, this was looked upon as very much my personal venture.

The board felt that the United Kingdom business was producing very good returns and they held the view that there seemed little justification for any speculative investment overseas. I was realistic enough to be aware that there were shareholders to consider, and I had to live with the fact that I could not always rely upon my intuitive judgement being backed by hard cash.

My personal stake was roughly equivalent to the money put up by each of the corporate investors. The publicity created by this new venture quickly seized upon the fact that it was me, not the public company which bore my name, that was taking the risk inherent in such new developments.

Pontinental was never a public company, but my reputation in the City of London was sufficient to persuade certain members of the Stock Exchange to create a very limited, but active market in the shares. Before very long the one shilling (5p) shares were changing hands at prices up to 13 shillings (65p), which caused me to issue a statement which stated that I deplored the practice.

The early results could not possibly justify such capital appreciation and, if matters were not checked, I felt that there could be a ticklish, and possibly a damaging sequel, to these transactions.

Fortunately, the Council of the Stock Exchange took action and barred all further dealings in the company's shares. The grounds for this were that there could not be a truly free market in shares of a company whose membership is limited to 50, as was the case with private companies at that time.

I am not sure of the position today, but it would be very unlikely that such a practice would even take place. I was flattered by the success of my earlier capital issues, but the speculation in Pontinental was embarrassing, especially in the light of what was to transpire in due course.

Sardinia, the second largest island in the Mediterranean, was the chosen location for the first Continental resort. The Pineta Beach Hotel at Platamona opened for business in 1963.

This was not to be without some fun and games on the day, when my first guests arrived by charter flight from the United Kingdom. It was a very important, if not an historic, occasion, as far as I was concerned, so I was determined to be there to meet them.

I also had to think quickly because I knew only too well that the building contractors were still laying the concrete in the main drive when I set off to the airport to welcome the new arrivals. There were many last minute jobs being done, so the longer the arrival of guests could be delayed the better as far as my somewhat frantic hotel manager was concerned.

Pineta Beach is on the north-west coast, only 20 miles from the airport at Alghero. Strictly speaking, there would normally have been little delay in getting everyone to their holiday destination. Some quick thinking was called for. I decided to greet everyone by announcing that as they were the first of my guests to Sardinia it seemed only fitting to arrange for the coach driver to show them all just how attractive the island was. Also to give them a taste of the local wine.

We set off on what was to prove to be an extensive tour. I am afraid that because of the difficulties back at the hotel I gave instructions to proceed around the island until such time as the order was given to head for the hotel.

One sharp-eyed client spotted a building he had already seen and exclaimed: 'We're going round in circles, we've been here before'.

I replied that he must be mistaken and added : 'All these foreign places look the same'.

There had to be a time when matters could be delayed no longer. As a result, when they climbed out of the coach at the new hotel they left footprints in the concrete, though they found a warm welcome when they got inside.

They all knew that they were the first clients and took our many teething problems in their stride. I did not try to cover all of the inadequacies and did my best to offer compensation by some free rounds of drinks.

It is worth recording that the original manager at Pineta Beach, Franco Tresoldi, is still there. He has proved to be the best and most consistent manager in the entire Pontinental operation, although there have been other successful people to undertake these most demanding duties.

Despite the sale of virtually all of the Pontinental hotels and holiday villages, the bulk of which now operate as HCI (Holiday Club International), Pineta Beach is still owned by Holiday Club Pontin's and is offered as an alternative to the UK centres and holiday villages. There is now a 150-bedroomed hotel, complete with swimming pool and sun terraces with some attractive self-catering bungalows nearby.

There is also a fine white beach backed by scented pine groves. I am absolutely delighted that the first of my overseas ventures has remained within the organisation.

Ann Miller always had a special affection for Pineta Beach and she took a special administrative interest in the resort. In this context she would now be interested to know that the majority of the visitors to this particular attraction emanate from Italy as well as several west-European countries.

British guests now form the minority. There has been a turning of the circle from the original intention, but I would also like to feel that my foresight in placing such a significant investment in the island as early as 1962 was completely justified.

On reflection, it must have been the challenge of making a success of the entire concept of Pontinental which fascinated me. It was very hard work and many mistakes were made.

There were great difficulties in recruiting the right people and also in comprehending the local issues. Solving – even ignoring – planning problems, dealing with errant building contractors, pure naivety and tolerating bureaucratic nightmares were part of my daily life in the early part of the 1960s.

I must have been a glutton for punishment, especially as I did not have the customary consolation of the unanimous support of the board, the main opposition being led by Tim Moorcroft, who was previously with Butlins and may have remembered Billy's unfortunate experience in the Bahamas.

Each member could see that I was spending a great deal of my time in dealing with all of these matters, but, despite this, they did not attempt to curtail my activities. On the other hand, they saw no attraction in exercising Pontin's option to subcribe for new capital in Pontinental. It was, however, arranged for the necessary date to be extended, mainly on my recommendation and expressed optimism that one day all would come good.

Pontin's did not become financially involved with the overseas operation until the end of 1964, when they loaned up to £350,000 on a short term basis to cover Pontinental's capital commitments for developments already in progress.

I gave my personal guarantee that this money would be repaid by 31 March 1965, which was somewhat out of character, because I was not too keen to set this type of precedent in connection with an investment I did not absolutely control.

In my annual statement to Pontin's shareholders I undertook to supply the latest trading results for Pontinental in early 1965 and also promised to convene a special meeting before any decision was taken in respect of the exercise of the option.

By that time Pineta Beach was operational and the 1965 brochure was also offering the newly-constucted hotel S'Agamassa at Santa Eulalia del Rio, Ibiza, which was managed by my son-in-law, Peter Hopper and my daughter Patricia. The holiday village in Cala Mesquida, Majorca, had also opened in 1964.

We had reached a stage then where Pontin's needed to extend the scope of its booking facilities, which were traditionally handled at the site of each operational unit. Our advertising budget was growing in each successive year and the results of this increased exposure on TV, in national newspapers and various journals demanded easier access by the public.

I opened an information and retail travel office adjoining Oxford Circus in the West End of London and a similar bureau opposite Liverpool Street Station in the City. These premises also undertook all manner of travel business, as well as receiving bookings for our own centres, which again was a new departure for the company.

The Oxford Street building also had the benefit of a private cinema. This was used to show colour films of the activities at UK and Mediterranean holiday resorts. The screenings took place on a daily basis throughout the booking season and proved to be a great success.

These facilities were also of great assistance to me when I was seeking to impress stockbrokers, institutional investors and the company bankers. Our image was being transformed and was analogous to our growth. We were approaching the time when we would be matching Butlins virtually bed for bed, and our smaller units were still proving to be very attractive to our long-term clients.

Overseas, however, I still had a lot to do. My problems were by no means over. Despite my earlier assurances to the board and the shareholders, Pontinental was not coming good, though I was not losing faith and continued to back my judgement by further personal commitments.

I will comment upon the effect of the lack of confidence by my colleagues a little later, but it did not please me to have to report in my annual statement that the Pontin's loan to Pontinental had been increased to £500,000 and repayment delayed to 30 June 1966. This extra money would not have been made available without my own guarantee, so I gave it on the basis that it served to increase my determination to succeed.

Business at home was going from strength to strength meanwhile, and annual profits were approaching the magic total of £1 million following a period of sustained investment and expansion.

Pontin's option to subscribe for shares in Pontinental was extended again because the board would not sanction a permanent investment in their Chairman's overseas adventures.

It must be stated, though, that Pontinental would not have survived this period without the support of administrative staff at Pontin's UK head office. Apart from the loan arrangement, which was necessary to preserve the capital already invested by the shareholders, the admin back-up may not have been strictly official, but it was certainly forthcoming in terms of logistical support.

The situation could not continue on this basis forever, and in June 1966 Pontin's acquired the entire share capital of Pontinental against the issue of 4,200,000 Deferred Ordinary Shares . . . the equivalent to a price per share of 7$^{1}/_{2}$d in old money or 3.125p in decimal currency. This was at a discount on the original par value of 5p, but trading results could not possibly justify a higher figure.

Part of the deal was to rid ourselves of the Spanish partners, so the transaction involved the division of assets, although we retained the best sites.

The decision on Pontinental was more or less inevitable, given my personal commitment to justify the basis of the original investment, and I deeply regretted that the founder shareholders lost money on the deal. Those Pontinental shareholders who decided to retain their shares in Pontin's, however, eventually had a good run for their money later, when the group provided excellent returns. The deferred shares were converted to ordinary shares in April 1969.

I cannot say that my image was unduly tarnished by these matters, because it soon proved that my original policies were to be vindicated. In terms of my own investment, I also took a 'paper' loss, which I can attribute only to under-capitalisation for what was really a long term project.

It was too much to expect that Pontinental would produce immediate profits and – not for the first time – I learned from the experience.

In an effort to promote Pontinental I coined the phrase for the overseas holidays as 'Blackpool with the sun', but this did not really catch on. Mike Austin's present view is that although the overseas trading activities were an initial drain on domestic profitability, taking a long term view the parent company benefited enormously. It changed the image in terms of public view and perception of a company which was known for holiday camps that carried a down-market cachet.

Pontinental proved to be an exciting name, eminently marketable when package holidays were becoming more and more popular with the British public. Perhaps I was ahead of the market, but this will not prevent me from commenting that if I had received the full support of the board, right from the outset, the company would not have suffered from being under-capitalised and success would have arrived that much earlier.

Relieved of my personal obligations, and with the somewhat belated whole-hearted backing of my board and shareholders, I set about achieving a level of popularity for Continental holidays which I felt sure would guarantee success for the overseas holiday centres.

It must be remembered that in the mid-Sixties package holidays in Europe were still somewhat of a novelty as far as the mass market was concerned. Pontin's regular clients were inclined to be rather timorous about unorganised holidays abroad, but I was able to convince them that Pontinental was an entirely different matter.

They had learned to trust me at home and it was not long before they were displaying judgement in my favour for places farther afield.

The UK business was by no means suffering from the competition offered by Pontinental. If people were intent on going abroad, they would have been lost to Pontin's, anyway, so it made sense to offer the overseas alternative as part of the 'family' operation. Market Research also showed that the public were reacting more favourably to Pontin's on the basis that by having such attractive and exotic places abroad their sites at home must also have a lot to offer.

Although Pontinental had separate advertising material, the UK brochure also featured the overseas locations, which made it a much more attractive proposition. We obtained new business, especially from families with young children, and it was not long before the fuller range of our attractions was being translated into higher profits, although even when Pontinental became profitable the margins were below those of the domestic business.

At a time of currency restrictions our holidays abroad were looked upon as being cheap and competitive. I calculated visitors to Pontinental hotels and holiday villages would still have an adequate amount of spending money to take with them.

Nothing in this world can go completely smoothly, though. We had operational problems at Cala Mesquida on Majorca. This was formerly a camping site, operated and mainly frequented by Germans. Before I transformed it by adding 142 brick-built double chalets, shower blocks, dining room, kitchen and bar it was totally lacking in any modern facilities and services.

The approach road was nothing more than a rough track, but it was the lovely bay, clear blue water and wide beach which always captivated the new arrivals. Accommodation in those early days was pretty basic, though there were already plans to offer far superior apartments with en-suite facilities. It was absolutely essential that we should generate a high level of popularity.

There were no less than three managers, all of them English, during the 1964 season and I was wondering how we were going to face the summer of 1965 when Walter Rowley came to the rescue.

At the end of the 1964 season I arranged for all of Pontin's managers to be given a complimentary holiday at the Hotel S'Agamassa in Ibiza. I am told that this was looked upon as a gathering of the clans and a good time was had by all.

Walter had heard the gossip about a disastrous summer at Cala Mesquida and he volunteered to go and have a look with a view to taking over the manager's position for 1965. I was pleased to make the arrangements for him to take his family across on the ferry. Despite a rough crossing and a stay in an hotel with no electricity, he liked what he saw and decided to take up the challenge.

It was typical of Walter that during the winter he studied the Spanish language to overcome any problems in communicating with the large numbers of local staff. This was in addition to his duties in supervising the building programme.

He did a marvellous job and the new holiday village was ready when the first guests arrived. Before long guests from the UK were arriving in large numbers and I recall that in the 1965 season we were offering a return flight from Luton or Gatwick, two weeks full board, accomodation and free wine with lunch and dinner, as well as the organised entertainment for just £49 per person.

The drinks in the bar were also very cheap, again as a matter of policy. Walter proved to be an excellent manager and he stayed in the position for 8 years, during which period we further improved the resort and also added the nearby Cala Mesquida hotel to accommodate a further 180 guests in this increasingly popular location.

Walter always made a point of helping his guests to ensure that they got plenty of food by teaching them the Spanish word for more which is 'mas', pronounced 'mass'. He always got a laugh on the final night when he announced that he had received his usual weekly letter from the Pope which confirmed that there had been 'more masses said in Cala Mesquida than in all the churches in Spain'.

Walter likes to tell the story of the seaweed and how genial Fred Pontin worked a miracle!

The bay at Cala Mesquida was prone to regular inundation by a particularly obnoxious type of seaweed, which seemed to be influenced by wind and tide. One moment the beach and surf would be clear, but in no time at all the whole bay could be covered by a dreadful substance. It could hang around for days and sometimes weeks on end, quietly rotting on the shoreline and creating a dreadful odour.

The locals could offer no explanation for the phenomenon, but, as it tended to disappear as quickly as it arrived, everyone learned to accept a temporary inconvenience.

On one particular occasion, however, the weed arrived and considerable outstayed its welcome. I arrived at Palma airport and Walter met me by announcing that the guests knew that I was coming and were 'gunning' for me because they were furious that their holiday was being ruined by the state of the beach.

They felt that the management should be doing something, such as importing special equipment for a big clean-up operation – an impossible requirement for such a remote location on a comparatively small island.

I told my manager that I would meet a deputation after dinner and would do my best to calm matters, probably by offering a round of drinks.

I didn't get a chance. They were waiting for me as soon as I entered the bar.

Their spokesman came up and asked: 'Are you Fred Pontin?'

I replied that I was, and he asked what I was going to do about the seaweed.

'Why do you think I'm here? I've arrived specially to deal with the matter. I've arranged for all the necessary labour and machinery to clear the beach.

'The weed will be gone by the time you get up tomorrow morning.'

Walter looked at me in a very critical manner. He knew that I was booked out on a very early flight, and he would have to face the music.

'Do you mean that Mr Pontin?' said the guest.

'Of course I do.'

I was given not only a round of applause, but several drinks by guests who seemed absolutely convinced that all would be well if I said so.

There has to a happy sequel, otherwise the story would not be worth telling. A storm blew up that night and Walter remembers hearing the noise of the tide and surf growing louder every minute. The next morning the beach and bay were clear.

I couldn't wait to confront the spokesman from the night before and bask in the glory of my 'miracle'. Unfortunately, he couldn't be found and I had to be on my way to Madrid, en route to Heathrow, safe in the knowledge that poor old Walter didn't have to make any excuses on my behalf.

The guests were, of course, aware that nature came to the rescue, but they were very impressed that I could be so certain that it would happen on that particular night. Walter did nothing to break the spell, so it was 'Good Old Fred' for the remainder of their holiday.

Walter was a very special colleague. The one I turned to when I received my knighthood. I felt a need to share the aura which affected me at that rather auspicious time. I chose this special friend and loyal colleague, who joined Pontin's as a trainee manager in 1961 on leaving the army, where he had served as a Lieutenant-Colonel.

He had been told by an army chaplain, who had previously attended a Butlin's camp in an official capacity, that running a holiday camp was just like organising an army unit, so Walter responded to an advertisement in the *Daily Telegraph* and applied for a managerial position with Pontin's.

I took an instant liking to this new recruit and, after a short period of induction at Sand Bay, he decided to stay. He has been with the company ever since.

Walter was manager at Osmington Bay for three years, taking over from Ann Miller, who was appointed a director of the parent company. He then worked from our Bournemouth office on Pontinental matters before going to Majorca. He has undertaken duties as a public relations executive and nowadays he keeps his hand in by acting as a company consultant on special events, where his experience is invaluable.

As a most reliable colleague, I had no hesitation in asking him to travel up from Somerset to deliver my formal acceptance of the knighthood to number 10 Downing Street. I didn't go as far as to inform him of the contents of the envelope, which I had kept locked in the safe. I think he knew what it was all about and he was not surprised when the list was published on the Queen's Official Birthday.

I wanted him to be associated with the event and the visit to the inner sanctum of the Prime Minister was my way of achieving this aim.

I have highlighted Walter Rowley's success in Majorca to illustrate that efficient and friendly management was an absolutely essential ingredient for a successful site, whether it was in the United Kingdom or abroad. Pontinental was fortunate in having some outstanding managers, all of whom made important contributions to the eventual success of the company in its overseas operations.

I treated each Continental resort on the same basis as the centres in the UK. They all had regular visits from 'The Guv'nor' and the local staff became accustomed to my 'lookee, lookee' tours of inspection.

My empire was now very widespread. Because I liked to travel light, I made arrangements for several changes of my personal clothing to be available at each resort. I have always had a reputation for being smartly dressed, but this cannot be done if you are forced to wear a crumpled suit. I found that I needed only a briefcase when travelling abroad so I did not have to put up with regular baggage delays.

If I was going on my own it was usually necessary for me to travel on scheduled flights, but on frequent occasions I took any available opportunity to join my clients on charter aircraft if this did not prove to be too inconvenient.

I like to think that my Pontinental guests appreciated the boss travelling with them, eating the same food in the dining room and joining them for a drink in the bar both before and after the evening entertainment. I found myself joining in the fun and it all helped the 'family' image which became our hallmark over the years.

Another important personality in the development of Pontinental was my old friend Joe Rubido, who comes from north-west Spain. He used to run a pub in Hyde Park Square where I was a regular visitor in the mid-Sixties. At the time Pontinental was undergoing an important transitional period from trading losses and operational problems to the creation of a viable undertaking.

It was only natural that we should talk about the Spanish resorts which were under my control and the new development which was planned in Torremolinos. Joe took some persuading, but he joined the staff of the new hotel as assistant manager and was also put in control of the bars.

He arrived to find what he described as a 'building site', even though he maintains that I assured him that the hotel was ready. Perhaps I did, but he always knew that I was an optimist. When Joe gave the address of the hotel to the taxi driver he was told that he must have 'booked too early' because it was clearly unfinished.

Even then he was not totally prepared for the chaos which was causing my brother Len, who was supervising the building contractors, a few sleepless nights.

Nevertheless, the hotel opened on July 4 1970, when 500 guests arrived at what Joe insisted upon describing as a half-finished hotel. I was there at the time and must concede that the first guests had a lot to put up with, although I insisted upon letting everyone know that this was down to the building contractors, not ourselves.

On one occasion I became so frustrated at the lack of urgency which was being shown by the construction workforce that, when I saw a man filling a wheelbarrow with cement while another man watched with his hands in his pockets, I went over, grabbed a shovel, thrust it in his hands and told him to get on with the job.

He started working immediately, but you can imagine my surprise when that evening the same man came up to me in the bar and told me that I owed him a drink. He turned out to be a guest and had taken me literally, no doubt with his tongue planted firmly in his cheek. He got a few drinks and we had a laugh about Spanish construction workers.

I soon discovered that most of my overseas visitors were Pontin's clients of very long standing. They even described their hotel rooms as chalets!

Their loyalty to me and the company came to the fore when we experienced a strike by the local labour force. It was not just our establishment, most of the coastal hotels were similarly affected. Most of our guests set to work, made their own beds and, with the assistance of Joe Rubido and other managerial staff, a rota was set up. The hotel continued to operate on a virtually normal basis.

When the meals had been prepared by the chef, who was not one of the strikers, they were served by a party of guests, who would later join the others on the beach and around swimming pool, continuing with their holidays as if nothing was amiss.

One client insisted upon taking control of the Hobart dishwasher in the kitchen and would let no one else near it. By way of sustenance he was supplied with a case of wine, and he kept the machine going for hours on end until the strike was settled after a few days.

Other guests manned the bars, supervised entry into the dining room, cleaned the bedrooms, changed the linen and one particularly gifted engineer even fixed the lifts which had ceased to operate.

Thank heavens there were not too many strikes, but the one to which I have referred above was followed by a shorter one in the following year. Would you believe it if I tell you that the expert on the Hobart dishwasher just happened to be there? He again came to the rescue without a word of complaint.

I put this type of response down to team spirit created by people such as Joe Rabido, who seemed to have an incredible knack of getting people to do what he wanted. If there was any sign of trouble I would try to be there in order to take the brunt of the complaints or criticisms, but it was Joe who created the atmosphere which made my task that much easier.

He did go too far one evening, however, when he took the microphone to thank everyone for their assistance and co-operation. He went on to joke about the Spanish unions and said that they had caught the British disease by creating so many strikes.

One guest, who was a staunch trade unionist, took great exception to Joe's remarks and behaved in a very threatening manner. The situation was saved when another guest came to the rescue, took a swing at the complainant and shouted, to great applause: 'Don't you be rude to our Joe!'

After these strikes I thought it only right and proper that my guests should be compensated for the inconvenience. Each was given a £50 voucher towards the following year's holiday.

I took a similar line in rewarding the UK staff with 'free' Pontinental holidays if I became aware that there were any empty seats on the chartered aircraft to the various resorts. This was not unusual in the off-peak season and the staff appreciated the gesture.

Joe and I once travelled to Malaga to purchase a set of drums for one of the hotel's entertainments staff called Vic Bickers, who was marvellous at his job of entertaining the children. He had been pressing for drums for some considerable time. He said that the guests could then enjoy him accompanying the very talented pianist who performed every night in the main bar.

Joe was certain that Vic had no idea how to play the drums, but I became so bored with the constant lobbying that I agreed to supply what was needed and, in any event, it would make a pleasant day out with my old friend.

Joe was right. When we got back to the hotel Vic could not even set up the newly-purchased instruments of percussion and, when he eventually succeeded in creating some form of structure, it was clear that his talents lay elsewhere.

He was going through the motions without making a sound and in the meantime the pianist ignored him. We were making catcalls from the bar 'Come on Vic, let's be having you', but not even a whisper was heard. Vic never touched the drums again and they became somewhat of a white elephant, but at least it stopped his continual pleading.

People say that I have been too soft in dealing with that type of case, but, if certain individuals were good at their jobs, and Vic certainly came into this category, I saw no reason why they should not be allowed to indulge themselves on the odd occasion, especially if it did no one any harm.

These were, however, impulsive gestures on my part and no

member of the staff could be absolutely sure how I would respond to any other requests.

Joe's first season at Torremolinos was intended to be his last as far as he was concerned. The hotel closed at the end of October and the winter was spent in finishing it off properly. He told me that he had had enough, he was worn out, it was too hot and he found difficulty in understanding the southern Spanish dialect.

He had been in the UK a long time, but it still seemed peculiar that he appeared to hate his native country. He once complained that he had a severe attack of 'Montezuma's revenge', when he went back to spend a short holiday in his home region.

I had a job on my hands in persuading him to return. It took many pints at the Highland Bar in Hyde Park Square before Mike Austin and I persuaded him to go back at the start of the following season. He said that this was very much against his will, but I am pleased to say that he stayed for eleven years and played a great part in making Torremolinos into a very successful hotel.

By owning the Pontinental resorts, Pontin's had created an extra dimension to its business. By the early 1970s the demand was exceeding supply as far as the overseas sites were concerned.

I had planned to double the occupancy at Torremolinos to over 1,000 beds and, in due course, I even went as far as to anticipate formal planning permission. New attractions included an indoor heated swimming pool, grill room and conference facilities, because I was convinced there was business to be had during the winter months.

I built extra accommodation for 120 guests at the Cala Mesquida Hotel, which was re-named Hotel Pontinental and then became an important and successful adjunct to the holiday village centred around the ever popular bay. Sardinia had also been the subject of expansion, but it was not until 1972 that I negotiated a deal which succeeded in providing an additional 4,200 beds at one stroke.

Pontinental acquired S.A. Holiday Club, a Belgian group operating six holiday villages in Majorca, Spain's Costa del Sol, Morocco and Greece. This timely acquisition not only gave us the extra beds and improved our range of sites for Pontinental's British market, but also put us in a position of considerable strength as far as the overseas holiday market was concerned.

Over half of the additional beds were being sold through Belgian, German, French and other European tour operators. This deal put the Pontin's group of companies into the major league and well ahead of the British competition – and any other European operator.

I now felt confident that my dreams of creating a truly international holiday empire had been realised. Moreover, I was able to emphasise that our overseas investments provided financial security to the British holiday-maker, allied with complete control of accommodation and service. Our customers knew what to expect and they were not disappointed.

No one now talked about Pontinental's 'problems' – only their successes. I was beginning to ask myself if there were any new mountains worth climbing.

It was not long before City Editors and financial journalists in the national Press were speculating about the future of Pontin's, but not because there were doubts concerning its stability or its long term prospects. It was really the line of succession which seemed to provide the fascination.

I had now passed my seventieth year and, although I had never mentioned the word 'retirement', it was inevitable that there would be talk about the likely candidates for taking over a business with annual profits of around £7 million, earned from a turnover which was then approaching £50 million.

I will not deny that I had let be known that a bid would be successful if the price was right, but I also had my own views on the type of company which would be best-suited to safeguard the interests of a loyal staff and to take Pontin's into the 1980's.

To this day I am flattered and sometimes embarrassed by the fact that many of Holiday Club Pontin's guests are still under the impression that I have remained at the helm of the company. This may, or may not be due to the fact that when Trevor Hemmings and his team succeeded in negotiating the management buy-out of Pontin's from Bass in 1987 they were kind enough to appoint me to the strictly non-executive post of Founder President of the company.

This was a touchingly generous gesture, which served as a form of compensation for previous disappointments.

Only three general managers have survived my own regime at Pontin's: Eddie Stamper at Osmington Bay, David Gwyn at Pakefield and Pat Braden of Plemont Bay in Jersey, who started out as a Blue Coat.

It is fitting that it is this particular trio which has remained with the business. Each typifies the special breed of men who become what can only be described as 'infected with the fascination' such a career provides.

As President of the company I still keep in touch with the group's activities, but my visits to individual centres are now very rare, unless there is some special occasion, such as a visit to Ireland when a vastly improved Trabolgan was brought back into the fold.

I was also invited to the special celebration the twenty-first anniversary of the British Red Cross Society week in Pakefield.

I have never been too surprised by my popularity with the guests, because I have gone out of my way to create a high profile within the business. Appearances in the dining room, ballroom, and, more popularly the bar, were commonplace both at home and abroad. In that respect I could never be compared with that fictitious, but always absent proprietor of holiday camps, Joe Maplin, in the already-mentioned popular BBC TV programme *Hi-De-Hi*.

It is rather satisfying that I seem to occupy a modest place in the treasured memories of at least a cross-section of the hundreds of thousands of my guests over the years. I know this because I received sacks full of letters telling me so.

*Chapter Eleven*

# ARISE SIR FRED

THE CITATION indicated that my knighthood, which was announced in Her Majesty the Queen's 1976 Birthday Honours List, was awarded for charitable services.

Although I had been personally active in this field of activity for many years, my main energies in this respect had been channelled through my membership of the Variety Club of Great Britain, into which – on the introduction of Albert Stevenson – I was admitted as a Barker in 1966.

The next year I was very pleased to be asked to join the 'Crew', in other words the organising committee. In the following year I was astonished to be nominated for Chief Barker by the late Jimmy Carreras, Variety's International Chairman, who also received a knighthood for similar charitable services.

I was then elected to succeed Sefton Myers, who was a tower of strength in his year of office during which the Variety Club raised an all-time record sum of £685,000 under his leadership.

Variety in this country is known mainly for its world-famous Sunshine Coach Scheme, which supplies vehicles to charitable organisations connected with the welfare of handicapped and under-privileged children throughout Great Britain and the Channel Islands. These vehicles can be high-top mini-coaches or even larger coaches, which cost more than twice as much to supply in a fully equipped manner.

The coaches are delivered to such grateful recipients as hospitals, children's homes, boys' clubs, spastics societies, Dr. Barnardo's Homes, special schools and to branches of the British Red Cross Society.

The Club also responds to countless requests for other forms of charitable contributions to literally thousands of children who are short of warm clothing and toys at appropriate times during each year.

There are various funds and campaigns within the organisation, such as the Heart Fund and the Christmas Toy Campaign. The full nature of the Club's entire range of activities are strongly supported by many members of the show business fraternity as well as business tycoons and entrepreneurs such as myself.

Numerous social and fund-raising functions took place throughout the year. It was through Variety Club activities that I became acquainted with members of the Royal Family, such as His Royal Highness the Duke of Edinburgh, the late Earl Mountbatten of Burma, both of whom held gold card life memberships, Her Royal Highness Princess Alexandra and the Hon. Angus Ogilvy.

The role of the Chief Barker is to spearhead the Variety Club's efforts to raise the money needed for its work and I set about my task with even more energy than I was accustomed to generating for my business activities. I travelled all over the United Kingdom attending as many functions as I possibly could.

During my year of office there were celebrations marking the 50th Anniversary of the Royal Air Force and the 25th Anniversary of the Royal Air Force Association. One of the highlights was a Variety Club luncheon at the Savoy Hotel, where Prince Philip was Guest of Honour. This event was covered by BBC TV, ITN, Pathe News and the BBC Overseas Service, as well as the national Press, which ensured generous publicity for the work of Variety.

Nineteen-Sixty-Eight was a year that will always remain within my memory. My life was one long round of travelling and meeting people. With my holiday camps spread around the country the "coconuts" password would not have been needed if my managers had been fortunate enough to have had access to the itinerary for my duties with Variety Club.

If I was in the West of England I took the opportunity to pay what I have since discovered could be termed as promiscuous (look it up if you don't believe me) visits to as many of my centres as I could fit in. Everyone was kept on their toes.

The various managements were aware of the fact that this was a very special year for 'The Guv'nor', so their regular efforts towards charitable fund raising among staff and guests became more intense during the year.

Among the more memorable functions was a Sports Celebrities' Luncheon attended by 40 of Britain's most famous sportsmen, including Josh Gifford (National Hunt), Henry Cooper (boxing), Sir Alf Ramsey (football) Noel Murless (turf), Henry Cotton (golf), Stirling Moss (motor racing), and Roger Taylor (lawn tennis).

On March 12 I also chaired a luncheon at the Savoy Hotel which honoured 11 personalities selected for their outstanding achievements during 1967 in films, on TV, the stage, radio and records. Among the most notable recipients of Variety Silver Hearts were Irene Worth (Stage Actress), Warren Mitchell (BBC TV Personality), Dame Edith Evans (Film Actress) Kenneth Horne (BBC Sound Radio Personality) and a Special Award for the distinguished actress of the British theatre, Dame Gladys Cooper.

The Variety Club still holds an annual awards ceremony as part of what is often termed 'the congratulatory back-slapping season' for the entertainments industry. It is an excellent method of raising money and brings enormous publicity because the ceremonies are always televised on one of the national networks.

The host celebrity, almost invariably Terry Wogan in recent years, makes a point of featuring a generous plug for one of Variety's most deserving causes. This assists in the never-ending attempt to perpetuate public awareness when so many other charities are also competing for generous donations.

Members of the British public have always responded magnificently to appeal after appeal, and none more so than the hundreds of thousands of guests at Pontin's holiday centres over the last 45 years.

Variety's annual Members' Derby Sweepstake grossed an all-time record total of £87,600 at the Derby 'Stag' Dinner held in the Savoy on May 22nd and I very much enjoyed taking part in the draw. Variety's seventh annual Gala Greyhound Race at the White City stadium on the following Saturday attracted such stars as Diana Dors, Charlie Drake, Eric Sykes, and Roy Hudd.

I sponsored two races that night and I notice from the records that Prince Philip, a keen supporter of the Club's charitable activities, arranged for his own dog, Camira Flash, to compete in the Sir Billy Butlin Stakes. Unfortunately for H.R.H., it was beaten by Yellow Printer, which set up a new course record for the distance.

I have had many an enjoyable night at the 'dogs', and none more so than when I was privileged to be accompanied by Prince Philip at Clapton Stadium during that same year. This was shortly after he and I had attended a tea party and commissioning ceremony at the London Hospital, where I had presented a new heart machine in gratitude for my recovery from a serious motor car accident. This was their first heart machine and it is still in use today, although there have been modifications and improvements over the years.

I am not sure if Prince Philip had never been to a no-frills greyhound meeting before, but he did not surprise me when he responded to my suggestion in such a positive manner, because I had been told that he was fond of taking a break from his normal routine.

The Royal Family is known for not carrying any money, but there was no problem on this particular occasion as he showed no inclination to have a bet, even though I had two of my own dogs running that evening. Prince Philip was more interested in savouring the atmosphere.

This memorable year continued with Variety's 15th annual Star Gala at Battersea Park Festival Gardens. The event was sponsored by the *News of the World* to benefit the Heart Fund. Despite occasional showers of rain, the fans turned out in their thousands to meet their favourites from screen, stage, television and discs, including Tony Blackburn, Judith Chalmers, Liz Fraser, Dickie Henderson, Richard Todd, Robert Morley and band leader Joe Loss.

Variety was honoured during May by the presence of Bob Hope at the tribute luncheon to the record industry held at the Savoy. Bob sat on my right-hand side and I recall that he seemed desperately tired after an all-night flight to London. He was still voted an absolute 'wow' by the 480 assembled guests, who included a then-bearded Harry Secombe, Sandie Shaw, Jimmy Tarbuck, Victor Silvester, Max Bygraves and Jimmy Young.

It was my duty to chair the luncheon, though you can imagine how relieved I was not to have to follow Bob Hope. Announcing him was nevertheless a daunting task because any joke would appear inadequate in front of such a master, but I managed to survive the ordeal and hopefully raised the odd smile.

Bob cracked a couple of jokes about Harry Secombe's weight and went on to allege that he himself had tried to cash in on the pop record market, but instead of winning a golden disc for selling a million records he was given 'a golden hole for selling none'. He was being modest – everyone knows that *Thanks For the Memory* has sold hundreds of thousands of copies and is known throughout the Western world. Bob's address was preceded by Norrie Paramour giving his own piano rendition of the comedian's theme song.

*A family reunion in 1958. Sister Elsie, Harry, Mother, myself and Len.*

*My racing triumph – leading in my 1971 Grand National winner Specify.*

*A chance to meet Mrs Mary Wilson at a No. 10 reception.*

*One of my perks – 'working hard' at a Miss Pontin's final.*

*Greeting one of my heroes, Lord Mountbatten.*

*A Variety Club happy occasion with Prince Philip.*

*H.R.H. Princess Margaret's smile greets my bow.*

*Raising money with H.R.H Princess Alexandra.*

*Charlie Drake fights with me over Diana Dors.*

*A moment that terrified me – walking alone into the spotlight at a Royal Albert Hall reunion.*

*Manny Shinwell (rt) and I with Jack Solomons when he received his O.B.E.*

*A precious souvenir, Manny Shinwell's salver.*

I have never been a natural public speaker, though with many company annual general meetings behind me, not to mention my annual 'spot' at the Pontin Reunions, I had been getting in plenty of practice. Starting 'cold' was always a problem, but after the odd drink I managed to get into some form of stride and people were always very kind, even if I had an 'off day'.

I was sometimes disconcerted to see my speech referred to as a 'charming address'. In estate agent's parlance this is a euphemism for something entirely the opposite, but I learned to concentrate on putting on a good show and not to let the side down.

Representing Variety in distinguished company was an undoubted honour and I am pleased to recall that my natural confidence played a significant part in my successful year in office.

My biggest test at speech-making came when Prince Philip was guest of honour at a private dinner-party given by the Executive Board and Crew at the Dorchester Hotel on Thursday, February 29th, 1968.

It fell to me to propose the toast to our Royal guest . . . I hope I carried it off to everyone's satisfaction, including H.R.H.

Other features of my 'Variety Year', were Royal World Premieres of two films which are still regularly shown on TV some 20 years later. These were *Chitty Chitty Bang Bang* and Lionel Bart's *Oliver*. I felt overwhelmed by the splendour of these occasions. *Chitty* 'the most fantasmagorical musical entertainment in the history of everything' was screened in the presence of Her Majesty The Queen at the Odeon Leicester Square. The premiere of *Oliver* had earlier received the endorsement of H.R.H. Princess Margaret and the Earl of Snowdon, who were accompanied by the Prime Minister, the Rt. Hon. Harold Wilson and his wife Mary.

The numbers of famous film stars attending these spectacular occasions were enormous. I found that it was difficult to keep up with what was going on because my eyes were wandering in several different directions at the same time.

*Chitty* was also part of a quite breathtaking feat of organisation. Arrangements were made for the simultaneous 12-city World Premiere of Albert R. Broccoli's temporary diversification from his James Bond movie productions, but even I could not be in all of the venues at the same time.

All were held on the same day as the London showing – December 16th – and the film was exhibited to distinguished audiences from every principal town and city in the United

Kingdom from Glasgow to Brighton. Variety was to benefit from every triumphant performance.

It is fitting to mention that this mammoth project, the most ambitious of its kind ever undertaken in the UK at that time, was initiated by Variety Crewman Kenneth Winckles, who was then Managing Director of United Artists, but formerly with the Rank Organisation, whose Odeon theatres were an essential element in the operation. Star interviews from the Odeon Leicester Square were relayed nation-wide by closed circuit television.

My year of office as Chief Barker created a new record in terms of raising money. The figure comfortably passed the £1 million mark for a single calendar year, but I was the first to concede that it was the teamwork which produced such exceptional results. I was also fortunate to be involved with such a tremendous programme of activities.

Bernard, now Lord Delfont, succeeded me as Chief Barker in 1969, when I was honoured with the title of Elder Statesman and presented with a gold life membership card, which I shall always cherish. Bernie's year in office started with a bang at the annual dinner-ball at Grosvenor House, Park Lane, when the proceeeds grossed yet another all-time record of £60,000 – overtaking my own figure from the previous year.

Bernard was also awarded his peerage in the Birthday Honours List of 1976, which was a nice 'double' for Variety, as well as for the Grand Order of Water Rats of which we are both Companion Rats. Other notable Companion Rats are their Royal Highnesses Prince Philip, the Prince of Wales and Prince Michael of Kent.

The work of the Grand Order, of which the late Bud Flanagan was a founder-member, is very much associated with charitable causes closely  linked to the entertainments industry. Membership is very exclusive and I am proud to have been a member for many years.

Also that year a fellow-member of Saints and Sinners – another exclusive club, where membership is limited to 100 members – Group Captain Douglas Bader received his knighthood, so I was in distinguished company.

Although the club was not formed as a charitable organisation, over the years it has donated many tens of thousands of pounds for good causes. Co-founders were Percy Hoskins, former chief crime reporter of the *Daily Express,* and Jack Hylton, the famous impresario. One of the latest vacancies was filled by Sir Denis Thatcher.

Arthur Lewis MP put my name forward for my own knighthood and I was rather flattered when he told me that he had performed this service for only two other people: Sir Charles Clore and Sir Isaac Wolfson, both of whom were well-known benefactors on a very large scale, especially to Jewish charities. I knew Arthur through my membership of Jack Solomons' World Sporting Club.

Another political friend who joined me in my love for boxing was 'Manny' Shinwell, Companion of Honour and a long-serving and very distinguished Member of Parliament, who was elevated to the House of Lords after being a member of the House of Commons for almost 50 years, being a junior minister as early as 1924.

I took the chair at the celebration of his 90th birthday, when a dinner was held in his honour at the Grosvenor House Hotel under the auspices of the World Sporting Club on 21 October 1974.

If I was ever to be overawed by a distinguished gathering, this had to be it. This spectacular occasion was attended by no less than five former British prime ministers, two of whom are no longer with us. These eminent guests were Lord Avon (formerly Sir Anthony Eden), Harold Macmillan, Sir Alec Douglas-Home, Harold Wilson and Edward Heath. Other noteworthy parliamentarians included Selwyn Lloyd, the then Speaker Elect of the House of Commons, who gave the first speech in honour of a most warm-hearted and genial friend.

The best speech was given by Harold Wilson, who, after addressing me as 'Chairman Fred', as opposed to the 'more formidable Chairman Mao', struck just the right note. I remember his quip that in the knowledge that Manny had married again just the year before and at the age of 88, many of his friends who knew him had come to the conclusion that he 'probably had to'. This brought the house down, with much table-thumping and Manny laughing more than the rest of us.

Harold Wilson presented Lord Shinwell with a silver salver, which was engraved with the signatures of many of the distinguished guests, including that of each prime minister alongside my own. The next morning I received a telephone call from Manny, who said that he would like me to buy the salver for the sum of £5,000. He wanted me to send the money to a list of his nominated Jewish charities.

It was impossible to argue with such a personality and on such a delicate subject. He was determined not to keep the gift on a shelf or in a cupboard. He wanted it to be associated with acts of benevolence and compassion to others.

I readily agreed to purchase the silverware and sent off a number of cheques, each in the name of Manny Shinwell, to his favourite charities. It is not generally known that this was the fate of the commemorative gift given with such great affection on behalf of all present on that great occasion. I still have the salver and will have to consider its future in due course.

Manny was a unique character, who more than deserved the tributes made on that memorable evening. He did, of course, live to be over 100 years of age. When he achieved this significant milestone he spent nearly two hours in shaking the hands of one thousand admirers at a Parliamentary reception. Many there had been his political opponents yet counted him as a lovable adversary. I recall being with him just a day or so before he died and found his vigorous character very much in evidence to the every end.

The late George Brown is also a character to be remembered. I met him at that celebratory lunch. There was some light-hearted banter between the three of us and I was flattered by the remark that I should have been in the House of Lords, where my knowledge and experience would have been very useful.

No-one took the hint . . . but it is probably just as well because I am not sure that 'Baron Pontin of Bracklesham Bay' would have gone down too well with my clients! The knighthood raised more than a few eyebrows in the bars of the Pontin's camps. Perhaps my image as a man of the people was slightly dented.

Looking again at charitable activities, the British Red Cross Society has always been one of my favourites. I regard the international organisation, of which it forms part, as the leading charity of the world.

It has been my privilege to support many good causes and appeals over the years, but the Red Cross always figured prominently as recipients for what I have been fortunate enough to be able to contribute on a personal basis, as well as through the company.

I was sought out in 1960 by the Director of the Dorset branch of the Red Cross Society, Miss Norah Branigan, OBE, and I am indebted to her for being able to record some of the history of Pontin's association with such a worthwhile cause.

Norah and her committee hit upon the idea of organising a brief holiday for disabled young people and residents in hospitals for the elderly. She started out in 1954 by persuading Dorset County Council to lend her a former Children's Home in Dorchester, which she furnished and equipped by exploiting every conceivable source of goodwill from friends and colleagues.

Only very small numbers could be accommodated on this basis. After continuing the process for five successive years she decided that the results were so worthwhile that efforts should be made to repeat the exercise on a national basis.

She came to see me and I agreed to make the entire accommodation at our Riviera chalet hotel in Weymouth available to the Red Cross at half the normal rate. For two years this Weymouth venue became a holiday resort for disabled people from all over the country until, as a result of a change in policy, future guests were from Dorset only.

These weeks were such a great success that in 1963 Red Cross National Headquarters contacted Norah to see if she would sound me out on the subject of running a National Camp for disabled people. We had a meeting with national officials and it was agreed that our Blackpool camp would be an ideal venue for up to a thousand disabled people, accompanied by sufficient numbers of helpers.

This inaugural national week took place in October 1963, not in the best of weather conditions but everyone was thrilled by a visit from Princess Alice. Another venue for the Red Cross has since been Pakefield. These weeks started in 1971 and are still taking place – with David Gwyn, the manager, catering for some 800 visitors and helpers each year.

The Dorset holidays at Riviera have continued to the present day. From 1968 I was able to arrange for Pontin's to waive all charges, thus releasing branch funds for other equally worthwhile causes. All the Red Cross has to do is to cover the cost of travelling and the transfer of equipment. Everything else is free, and I am delighted to report that successive owners of Pontin's have continued their support by heavily subsidising these annual events.

The British Red Cross Society has always had a tireless body of workers without whom these weeks could never take place. I know that as far as Dorset is concerned Norah Branigan would like me to single out Heather Walters, who has been associated with the Riviera holidays from the outset. I must also mention Ann Miller in this context, because over a period of many years she bore the brunt of the close liaison that was absolutely essential for the success of these rewarding occasions.

I do not support these very worthwhile causes in order to obtain rewards, but I was immensely honoured to receive what Norah has described as the 'highest grade' of the British Red Cross Society's Badge of Honour. I shall treasure this for the remainder of my days.

They say that charity begins at home. Bearing in mind that the Borough of Christchurch is very close to Bournemouth, where Pontin's maintained its head office for many years, it should not be surprising that there were occasions when I did my best to help the odd local cause throughout the 1960s.

We started a long association with the town in 1962, when we received planning permission, at the third time of asking, for the holiday camp at Wick Ferry. Over the years I was able to associate myself and the business with a wide range of local charitable activities.

It was a chance remark in 1968 by the Mayor, the late William Bridge, that led me to donate an official coat of arms to the Borough.

The mayor had remarked that the item suspended from his chain of office was merely a replica of the old borough seal and not a coat of arms, because none existed. I saw an opportunity to make a popular gesture, offering to pay for what would be necessary to produce the armorial ensigns by the Richmond Herald. There followed a long period of local consultation until a final design and the motto *Fidelity and Freedom* were agreed.

I was presented with a fine painting of the armorial ensigns in January 1971, when I was amused to read a report in the local paper reporting that King Alfred had never thought of giving a coat of arms to his Royal Borough: this was left to Fred Pontin, 'which must be classed as a singular piece of one-upmanship!'

The painting was once displayed in the reception area of Wick Ferry Holiday Village, but it has now been restored to my personal possession. I was more than pleased that Ann Miller accompanied me when the borough presented me with the painting, because she did so much to assist me in achieving a particular level of status three years later.

I had no idea that all of this would lead to me being admitted as an Honorary Freeman of the Borough of Christchurch. But it did, and the ceremony took place on February 5th 1974, when I was presented with a casket containing the Scroll recording the admission. I was overwhelmed by the honour and noticed the connection with the earlier event when I spotted that the Scroll, illuminated on vellum, included a colour reproduction of the Coat of Arms of the Borough.

*Chapter Twelve*

# POTTING BLACK

THE SUCCESS of any business is linked to input and cash flow. It doesn't matter how good you consider your product to be, if no one buys it you have no business.

Once it has been established that the customers are there and that demand can be satisfied, the next aim must be to ensure that the operational revenues are not too cyclical and become evenly spread throughout each financial year.

In some concerns this is not possible. Fireworks and Christmas crackers are good examples and the same has to be said about certain elements in the leisure industry. Way back in 1946 a season at Brean Sands was no longer than twelve weeks or so, but over the next three years this term was extended to cover a period of six months from Easter to October. It was the peak periods of the school holidays, though, which really ensured maximum occupancy.

With land and buildings remaining idle for six months, and with no appreciable revenue – advance deposits being the only form of cash return – it will be appreciated that my energies and those of my staff were being devoted to every conceivable form of innovation to prolong the operational season.

Some managers proved to be much better than others at this task. One or two eventually assumed roles which would rival the achievements of the more prosperous impresarios in the West End of London. I assure you that I am not exaggerating this aspect of their managerial activities, as I shall illustrate later.

I came up with the odd idea or two, but I cannot say that all of the suggestions put forward received my immediate blessing. Bob

Chapple and the ubiquitous Walter Rowley, in his new role as a public relations executive, were in the habit of using me as their sounding-board for what became known as Special Events. These were designed to be held at our various holiday centres during the off-peak seasonal periods.

Other holiday camp operators made efforts in the same direction: Ladbrokes, for example, specialized in conferences. Pontin's had an advantage in the overall exercise by having smaller-sized units and a wide geographical spread of the sites.

Ballroom dancing was an obvious activity that could be exploited to its full potential because this was one of the leading forms of entertainment in holiday camps just after the war. Ballrooms were invariably the first additional facilities after bars and restaurants had been constructed.

Our guests loved to dance to local and sometimes resident bands. It was, therefore, a natural progression to promote competitions leading to area and regional finals, then to the grand finals staged at Pontin's Annual Reunions. The reunions were first held at London's Seymour Hall, then, as the company grew in terms of volume of business, at the Royal Albert Hall.

It all started at Osmington Bay on the initiative of Ann Miller. The dancing festival organiser was, and still is, Mr Frank Mayne, who, with his partner Gladys Christopher, runs the Mayne Schools of Ballroom Dancing in Dorchester. In the business of promoting ballroom dancing he is known as the 'Quiet Man' and is held in the greatest respect. He received a well-deserved award from his peers in 1982.

These dancing competitions, over which presided the top adjudicators in the United Kingdom, were always treated very seriously. When the later stages were reached it was absolutely essential to employ some of the leading orchestras in the country.

National Finals almost invariably featured names such as Joe Loss, Ted Heath or Victor Silvester and to the present day these events still attract well-known musical ensembles, thus maintaining the highest possible standards.

The finals are now held in the excellent ballroom at Osmington Bay because the Royal Albert Hall Reunions ceased after Pontin's was acquired by Coral in 1978. Some of the greatest names in British ballroom dancing have appeared, or taken part, in Pontin's Dance Festivals, including Bill and Bobbie Irvine, thirteen times world champions, who often gave demonstrations.

Some of the more successful contestants, many of whom had started serious dancing only as a result of a holiday at Pontin's, went on to turn professional and even become world champions. Many such people commenced their dancing careers by joining the more experienced couples on the floor and, after gaining in confidence, by subsequently competing in the regular novice competitions staged at my camps.

Included in this select group are Stephen Hillier and Lindsey Tate. Others who turned professional were Keith Clifton with partner Judith Alston and Vic and Terry Marsden, who now live and teach in Spain.

From a pecuniary point of view it is pleasing to record that all of these events were attended by groups of loyal supporters, as well as the enthusiastic dancers, ensuring maximum use of our accommodation, bars and restaurants. On the other hand, it gives me enormous personal satisfaction to know that this purely commercial enterprise has led to the lives of a significant number of people being considerably enhanced. They, in their turn, have given so much pleasure to thousands of others.

The dancing festival is now in its thirty-second year and continues to attract competitors from not only the United Kingdom but all parts of the world.

It has been said that I was a pioneer as far as special events are concerned . . . and that others followed where Pontin's took the lead. This is undoubtedly true, but all we were doing was to discover the identities of leading enthusiasts for any given popular activity and offering them the best possible facilities for increasing the scope of their pursuits.

A good example of this is model-making and handicrafts, a suggestion which gave rise to great scepticism as far as I was originally concerned. I described it as 'kids stuff' when the suggestion was first discussed. I was persuaded to give it a trial and now Brean Sands has for many years hosted the 'World's biggest residential festival for model and craft enthusiasts'.

The popularity of professional snooker was undoubtedly created by colour television and BBC TV's programme *Pot Black*. In the early seventies we hit upon the idea of sponsoring a Pro-Am Snooker Festival held in May of each year at our Prestatyn Sands Holiday Centre, just after the World Championship had been decided.

Mike Austin was responsible for its promotion and he formed a Pontin's snooker committee, whose first members included the then World Champion, Ray Reardon, and Ted Lowe, the TV commentator.

The festival, which carried the incentive of big prizes, had two parts: a competition between eight invited professionals, who were all paid appearance money; and the Pontin's Open in which professionals took part in the closing stages against the amateurs, who had reached the last twenty-four after coming through five or six preliminary rounds.

The professionals were subjected to a handicap system devised by Ray Reardon and Ted Lowe. Each amateur was initially given thirty points in each frame, later reduced to twenty-one, the value of three blacks, when it became clear that the standard of the amateurs was higher than at first thought.

In 1974 the festival attracted, in addition to Ray Reardon, who won the professional tournament, such well-known names as John Spencer, John Pulman, Eddie Charlton, Graham Miles and Fred Davis. It was a great success. During the next two years the professional competition was won by Alex 'Hurricane' Higgins and Welshman Terry Griffiths respectively. In addition to the eight invited professionals, other 'pros' could take part as long as they were prepared to pay their own way.

The first winner of the Pontin's Open was a youngish amateur, also from Wales, called Doug Mountjoy, who beat Ray Reardon in the semi-final and John Spencer in the final round. He has never looked back since, even though he was to later confess that it was all he could do just to afford the cost of the holiday to compete in the tournament. It was obviously the best investment he had ever made in the whole of his life and he is now part of the Pontin's story.

The attraction, as far as the holidaymakers were concerned, was that snooker enthusiasts were able to mix with these great players, not only in competition on twenty-four top quality tables but also socially. All the well-known professionals were my special guests for that particular week at the Grand Hotel, Prestatyn, just across the road from the camp, which Joyce Hey, a long time friend and personal assistant, managed for two years.

I was an enthusiastic visitor to these popular snooker festivals, and not just to watch the flow of cash. Play was on a twenty-four-hour round-the-clock basis. We attracted maximum occupancy of 3,600 guests and had to turn many way because of the lack of space.

I also liked to watch the matches and mix with the players, both amateur and professional. It gave me great pleasure in later years when I saw how some of the young and gifted enthusiasts graduated to become not merely very successful but also World Champions. Steve Davis, with long ginger hair, won on his first visit to Prestatyn and John Parrott and Neal Foulds progressed from Pontin's Junior and Open tournaments to even greater rewards elsewhere.

Darts Festivals were also an obvious attraction. These were organised in association with the *News of the World* in the early days. This form of excitement took up no less than three tremendous weeks in each year. It all started at Brean Sands, but Camber Sands and Prestatyn were soon drawn into the new concept.

Very attractive prizes were on offer for men's, ladies and mixed competitions. Eric Bristow won his first major tournament at one of my camps long before he became World Champion. Other companies have followed us with this type of event, but we were the first – much to my great satisfaction.

I have played darts on only one occasion in my life. It was the day that I bought the camp at Bracklesham Bay in 1947 and I can only put it down to beginner's luck. I was playing a game in the local pub with the vendor, Joe Lyons, and Leslie Dean and George Harrison.

We were playing a game of 5001 against four of the locals. Towards the end of the game, with the locals needing only double one, it came to my turn to throw and the score needed was 157. We had to finish on a double and with just three successive darts I scored a treble 20, treble 19 and a double top!

They were all flabbergasted, but I protested that it was a complete fluke. The regulars, who had thought they were on an easy wicket, wouldn't play anymore, money having changed hands on the initial challenge. I was never tempted to enter any of my tournaments – it's always best to quit when you're ahead.

Pontin's were pioneers in advertising at football grounds, Blackpool having the foresight to allow us to have boards behind each goalmouth, bearing the slogans 'Go Pontin's' and 'Go Pontinental'. Because of my local connections, I tried to persuade the board to put their ground, which had development potential, up for sale. The facilities, particularly car-parking, were rather inadequate.

I thought that they would be well advised to apply the sale proceeds in  building a modern, out-of-town stadium, preferably near the motorway, thus attracting larger crowds. They were in the First Division in  those days, had won the FA Cup and had players of the calibre of Sir Stanley Matthews and Stan Mortenson.

Unfortunately they did not take my advice, but I enjoyed my early connections with the club, at one time being asked to join the board of directors. I also tried to persuade them to raise money by a public flotation on the basis that I would underwrite the issue but nothing ever came of my initiatives.

These football connections came to the fore in the early 1970's, when I came up with a scheme for organising Football Weeks. For an initial period of three years we brought together genuine supporters of famous football clubs in a friendly but competitive atmosphere, well away from the hooliganism which was already being experienced at some of the matches on Saturday afternoons.

We had a success on our hands again and the concept was extended in 1976 to a six-a-side football competition for junior players from the supporters clubs. With the help of Jimmy Hill, Pontin's negotiated a £90,000 deal with Ted Croker, Secretary of the Football Association, for a three-year sponsorship of the FA Charity Shield. This match, played at Wembley at the start of each season, was between the winners of the previous season's First Division championship and the FA Cup.

They were always televised, so Pontin's gained very valuable publicity as well as generous measures of goodwill.

Prior to this annual fixture we staged the final of the Pontin's Holidays six-a-side competition. What a thrill it was for these young players to play their match on the famous turf at Wembley Stadium. They seemed to be oblivious of the crowd growing bigger for the main event of the day. I felt very proud of all of them, especially those who went on to become full internationals.

We were assisted in all of the work which went on behind the scenes by some of the great names from the world of football, such as Bertie Mee, Bob Wilson, Lawrie McMenemy and Geoff Hurst.

My keen interest in the game dates back, of course, to the pre-war days at Walthamstow Avenue, but my connections with the Football Association usually resulted in some tickets for the big games, including the FA Cup Final. I watched it from a table in the restaurant, my usual companion being Joe Rabido, who is also a great fan. Having regard to my major sponsorship of football at youth and national levels, I was disappointed when tickets ceased to become available in later years.

Football coaching seemed to be a good idea in the early 1960's, so I engaged soccer stars of the calibre of Jimmy Armfield, now a radio commentator on the sport, Dave Mackay and John White, formerly of Spurs, as well as Ron Flowers of Chelsea, to undertake coaching sessions at camps in Devon, Suffolk, Sussex and on the Isle of Wight.

Former England captain Billy Wright was in charge of the operation and he did a great job on our behalf. It was not just the young lads who enrolled for these courses – there was also the occasional balding head, not to mention growing paunch, to be seen on the playing field.

Pontin's have enjoyed playing a leading role in the world of brass bands since 1974 and I have no hesitation in claiming credit for this innovation.

It all started on a Sunday afternoon at Southport Holiday Village, when I was surprised to see several hundred guests ignoring the beautiful weather by sitting in the ballroom listening to the Prescot Brass Band. I felt that if the music was so popular there must be scope for a special event.

On that particular day I did not need a lot of persuasion by Christina Lawton, secretary of the Prescot band, and David Gwyn, who was our Southport manager at the time, to put up prizes for a competition. Matters developed further when I met none other than the legendary brass band figure Harry Mortimer, CBE, at a Chelsea football match and the Pontin's Brass Band Committee was formed with 'H.M.' as musical consultant.

I had always felt that brass bands and Pontin's would be good for each other because we had perfect facilities for the annual championships, which are still taking place with over £25,000 at stake in terms of prize money and holiday vouchers.

There are senior and youth sections. Bands qualify at three regional venues over the Easter holidays before going forward to the Grand Finals at Prestatyn Sands in the last weekend in October. Approximately 200 bands compete in the Pontin's Brass Band Championship, all accompanied by thousands of supporters.

I knew it would be good for business, as well as the popularity of brass bands, and this has certainly proved to be the case. Moreover, the people involved are the most warm-hearted and generous you could ever wish to meet and I am honoured to have been involved with the movement. I hope they will not mind me adding that they were also good drinkers . . .

On the subject of music, Bob Chapple's great love is Country and Western, so festivals were started at several locations. These not only attract top artists, but give a chance for everyone to make the grade at properly organised auditions.

Eddie Grundy of *The Archers* could well have achieved his ambition to have been a big star if he could have persuaded his father to allow him some time off from Grange Farm to appear at Brean Sands, which is not too far away from Ambridge.

These popular events always attract large numbers of fans and maximum occupancy is virtually guaranteed.

This leads me to the 'impresario element' in the ranks of some of the more enterprising managers of Pontin's holiday centres. This particular form of creative activity has taken people such as David Gwyn, who started as an office junior and is now general manager at Pakefield, into show business in quite a big way.

His promotions feature jazz, *Sounds of the Sixties* and the *Big Bands,* all of which have more than a hint of nostalgia for his loyal fans. He attracts jazz bands with huge reputations, such as Mr Acker Bilk, Monty Sunshine, Ken Colyer and Kenny Ball and pop groups from the Sixties who are still going strong to-day.

The Searchers, Fortunes, Swinging Blue Jeans and the Rockin' Berries are names even I have heard of, and dance orchestras led by Ray McVay, Eric Delaney and Syd Lawrence are still firm favourites at Pakefield. These musical extravaganzas in the months of April, May, October and November have always been extremely well-supported, making important contributions to Pontin's out-of-season turnover.

David revels in the description 'Mr Big Band of Europe' and his enthusiasm continues to grow as each year passes.

It is impossible to write about special events without mentioning Christmas festivities at Pontin's. Certain of our sites were opened up for the Christmas and New Year periods from the early 1970s. From the outset we seemed to hit the right chord with our clients because we were always full. Mothers had no worries about having to cook the traditional fare if they wanted some time off from the kitchen, and there was no need to be involved with any drink-driving.

Entertainments staff and Blue Coats always arranged a very full programme of events to include music, carol concerts, dancing (ballroom and disco) and a range of professional cabaret acts to suit every taste. Any gaps were occupied by wrestling bouts, film shows, bingo, snooker tournaments and whist drives.

There was just about everything the guests were accustomed to enjoying in the summer season but with more time to enjoy what was on offer. All of this was a far cry from that very first time that a Pontin's camp opened for the yuletide festivities back in 1946

*Chapter Thirteen*

# END OF A DREAM

THE YEARS between 1978 and 1980 were two of the most confusing, hectic, and, at times, a bitter and very sad period for me and the company I had worked so hard to build up

Pontin's had changed hands twice in this time . . . first to the Coral Leisure Group and then to the brewing giant Bass, with other interested parties hovering around.

The company first merged in 1978 with the Coral Leisure Group, which included the Joe Coral betting shop business. In common with Ladbroke's, who had been buying up independent holiday camps since the early 1970s, Coral were to fall foul of the gaming laws in 1980, when they found their depleted cash flow could not service their heavy borrowings.

As Pontin's had often been described as the 'biggest free house in the United Kingdom', it seemed perfectly logical also that ownership should pass to a brewery. It was Bass which eventually moved in with an unconditional offer to acquire from the Coral group a business I had held so dear for many years.

Pontin's could no longer be described as a family company. Although the business continued to operate much as normal, given the continuity of middle management, the enterprise had lost its national figurehead when the holiday camp industry entered a phase of difficult trading conditions.

I had undoubtedly entered the business at an opportune time and, despite my all-to-often-expressed misgivings regarding the circumstances in which I relinquished managerial control of the company that still bears my family name. I probably left at the right time.

No person can go on for ever, but my greatest sorrow is that no one from my own family, my son-in-law or any of four grandsons, showed the slightest inclination to succeed me as Chairman and Managing Director. If, in dynastic terms, there had been an obvious successor it is reasonable to suggest that matters may have taken a different course.

The terms of the acquisition by Coral left me a rich man, but I was by no means ready for retirement. I have never really understood the meaning of the word, because I consider business as something to be enjoyed. The thrill of manipulating assets, whatever form they may take, is an activity which will always attract my interest. The thrill of the chase never fails to capture my imagination and I hope that it never will.

But, after the Coral involvement, I never really felt happy in the way 'my company' was going. I particularly felt responsible for my closest colleagues.

I found myself bidding farewell to my personal staff at the Oxford Street offices. Eileen Langridge had been my private secretary since 1975 and had performed the rather demanding duties in a highly competent manner.

We had our differences over punctuality, as she will readily admit, but she was always very loyal and could see that I was very unhappy with the turn of events. At the time I felt that everyone, including the majority of my own board of directors and Trevor Hemmings in particular, had turned away from me by becoming so closely associated with, and supportive of, Coral's managerial methods.

I now appreciate that this was inevitable. They could not serve two masters and Coral represented the future of the enterprise. The 'King' was certainly dead and I could not expect to have any significant influence over what was happening during the post takeover period.

It became very clear that I could never have countenanced any long term relationship with Coral in control of my company. I had no wish to be on the sidelines, so my mind turned to the immediate future. I would have liked to have retained the services of Eileen, but I could not justify her employment on a full time basis and I advised her to remain with Coral. She did not stay for too long, however.

After a period as a temporary secretary she applied for a job as secretary/personal assistant with an old friend of mine, boxing promoter Mickey Duff, and I was more than happy to give her an unqualified letter of recommendation. Mickey told her: 'If you were good enough for Fred Pontin, you are good enough for me'. Eileen has been a virtually indispensable member of his organisation for over eleven years.

Both she and her husband John have become fanatical boxing fans, having first become interested as a result of my association with Jack Solomons and the World Sporting Club. This is probably just as well, bearing in mind that she probably spends more than half of her waking hours in handling Mickey's extensive business affairs.

Eileen has said that she is very proud to have Sir Fred Pontin on her curriculum vitae. I must return the compliment by paying tribute to the way she looked after me at Oxford Street over a very stressful period of my life. She had been there when I received my knighthood and had seen how I presided over increasing company profitability, only to see me get involved with a sale which I came to bitterly regret.

I am sure, though, that her time with me was a valuable experience. I can only hope that her present employer does not follow a similar path. If he shows any signs of doing so I feel sure that Eileen will make him see the error of his ways.

To say that I was disappointed by the outcome of the events which took place in the early part of 1978 would be a considerable under-statement. I am now realistic enough to appreciate that I was in no position to exercise absolute control over the series of circumstances at the time. Events and decisions that led to the relinquishment of my influence over the affairs of a business that had transformed the lives of so many people over 30 years.

Not wishing to rely too heavily on the benefits of hindsight, I would now like to refer to some of the after-effects of the takeover of Pontin's and, at the same time, endeavour to impart a degree of circumspection in respect of my account of the course of events which led up to the sale in March 1978 of 'my company'.

It would be misleading for me to give any indication that I was becoming increasingly lethargic in my approach to a business which was then firmly established, both at home and abroad, with an extremely loyal band of clients.

There was still plenty to occupy my mind, even if it was not like the old days. I was more than a little irritated, though, when two members of my board, Bob Whitehead and Tim Moorcroft, sounded out the possibility of placing me on the sidelines not long after my seventieth birthday.

Their idea was for me to become 'President' of Pontin's with Whitehead as chairman and Moorcroft, of whom I had already thought of in terms of coming to the end of his career with the company, being appointed managing director. My instant reaction was to tell them: 'You must be joking!'

At a later date I came to appreciate that this was probably the time when the seeds were being sown for changes in future control.

On that occasion I felt it fitting that I should remind them that I had control of the board through my family and loyal ally, Ann Miller. It should be said that I heard no more talk on those particular lines, although my trusting nature was undoubtedly being put under a little pressure as a result of this incident.

In the meantime, Trevor Hemmings, had made his presence felt in more ways than one. He assisted in slimming down the operation where it was necessary and took part in negotiations with the unions. He reviewed our many sites and also examined other possibilities for expansion by acquisition. I had gathered together a very professional team of managers over the years, but as far as the board were concerned I had retained 'family control', yet there were never any serious disagreements among the directors.

I do not think that there will be too many raised eyebrows by these explanations, especially as research has revealed more than a little Press speculation in the mid-Seventies on the future of Pontin's and the intentions of the chairman.

The *Sunday Times* was rating the shares as a firm 'buy' and a good takeover prospect in November 1975. It made the point that the company was more than likely to fall into a corporate lap when the time came for me to retire. Derek Porter wrote in his column in the *Evening News* of the takeover rumours so often sweeping around my holiday camp empire and was astute enough to link these to a new consultancy agreement with the company.

Another national newspaper went as far as to list some of the starters in the Pontin's stakes at a time when our shares were changing hands at 27p. Allied Breweries, Bass, Thomas Cook and one or two of the so-called tobacco giants looking for diversification into leisure, were brought into the frame, but if market rumours were to be believed I was seeking a price of at least 40p for each share.

It is interesting to note that Bass were mentioned as long ago as 1976, but it was not until 1980 that they finally took the plunge and acquired Coral, which included Pontin's. That was after Grand Metropolitan had withdrawn from the fray, following a reference of their intended purchase of Coral to the Monopolies and Mergers Commission.

Bearing in mind that my business was so often described as the 'biggest freehouse' in the United Kingdom, it is difficult to comprehend why the breweries were so hesitant to place their accrued surpluses into family holidays. Although it is true to say that Grand Metropolitan, whose interests included the Watney breweries, had already acquired the late Harry Warner's group of camps.

Scottish & Newcastle are now heavily invested in Pontin's, Center Parcs and a quality time-share development. They are catering for an impressive cross-section of the market in a very competitive manner.

In the event, there had been a series of approaches to the company – the most serious being from the Ladbroke Group. I never took Ladbroke's Cyril Stein's intentions too seriously and, as I told George Ross Goobey at the time, I was not attracted to leaving Pontin's in the hands of an amusement machine and betting shop organisation.

This must leave the reader in some confusion, bearing in mind that it was Coral who were to be successful with their £56 million bid for the company in January 1978. Having regard to the passage of time, I am not sure that I am able to provide a definitive answer to what must appear to be an intriguing question, especially in view of my feelings of regret, even remorse, which arose from the biggest financial transaction of my entire business career.

At twelve minutes past three on the afternoon of 4 January, 1978 Pontin's shares were suspended at 38p 'pending an announcement', when the final stages of negotiations were taking place between me and Nicholas Coral, chairman of Coral Leisure Group. There had been abundant rumours concerning the identity of the bidder. Trust House Forte, EMI and Trafalgar House were among names mentioned, it being felt that we were too big for Coral to digest, even though they were capitalised at some £75 million before the acquisition.

The offer price, represented by a mixture of cash and Coral shares, valued each Pontin's share at 49p, thus putting a price tag of £55 million on my company. Some commentators felt that this was on the high side and that the deal might be resisted by Coral's shareholders.

On the strength of these comments the price of Coral shares fell by over 10%, thus devaluing the bid to a certain extent as far as Pontin's shareholders were concerned, but the matter proceeded to completion . . . not without many serious misgivings and second thoughts on my part.

In accordance with the merger arrangements I joined the board of Coral Leisure, together with Bob Whitehead, Trevor Hemmings and my son-in-law Peter Hopper, the latter mainly as a result of his Pontinental responsibilities. All of Pontin's board of directors retained their positions either on a fixed term basis or with provision for periods of notice.

In my case it was specifically stated that I would remain as Chairman of Pontin's only until 31 March 1980 and my appointment as Managing Director would expire after just twelve months.

It was my original intention not to have my name connected with the casino and bookmaking side of Coral, but my own directors insisted that I should join their management team to reassure Pontin's shareholders as well as the employees. I also signified my intention to stay in executive control of Pontin's for the full two years, with Coral not being in a position to interfere with the running of the company for at least twelve months. This was not to be. My suggestion that the merged group should be named Coral Pontin Leisure Group Limited also fell on deaf ears as far as Coral were concerned.

It was further stated in the offer document that a new Managing Director of Pontin's would be appointed when I relinquished the post, on the basis that Coral would by then have assessed what changes in management structure and style would be needed.

These arrangements should have persuaded me that my life was about to undergo a sea change of some considerable significance, but at the time I had other things on my mind, not least the continued doubts and uncertainties about the rationale of the entire transaction.

To complete the management structure for the merged businesses, Nicholas Coral and David Spencer, respectively Chairman and Financial Director of Coral Leisure Group, joined the board of Pontin's and Bob Whitehead and myself were also appointed to what was known as the Management Board of Coral.

Coral, already sensitive to its heavy reliance on earnings from gambling operations, had previously acquired control of Centre Hotels at a cost of some £17 million. The Pontin's purchase was considered as a move to take them into a much bigger league. This was achieved only by the doubling of their reliance on borrowed money to some £35 million, which left them in a state of some vulnerability when they eventually ran into trouble with their casino licences.

I am not going to dwell too much, though, on my association with Coral. The deal was officially represented as a merger between the companies, but was really a full scale takeover.

These were not particularly happy times for me. I felt uncomfortable. It was inevitable that I would resent the foreshadowed changes in managerial style and control. A lot of paper was flowing about, all from Coral's head office. The more I saw of it the more I regretted the so-called merger.

Something had to give. Following rather stilted negotiations with Michael Hoare, Coral's Managing Director, it was announced in October 1978, just a few days after my 72nd birthday, that I intended to resign as Chairman and Managing Director of Pontin's and as a director of Coral Leisure Group at the end of March in the following year. My sister Elsie and Ann Miller came to similar arrangements at the same time with our new masters. Son-in-law Peter Hooper also joined this mini-exodus from the merged companies.

Because at that time I was still firmly ensconced in the offices at 240 Oxford Street, Michael Hoare found it necessary to obtain my personal assurance that he would be able to establish a line of communication with Pontin's management. I suppose this fact speaks volumes on the atmosphere which was prevailing during the first season of operations after the takeover.

Arrangements for succession were being put in place, and my overall influence was diminishing by the day as far as the attitude of the Coral management was concerned.

News of my impending departure was not greeted with a great deal of surprise, bearing in mind the arrangements disclosed at the time of the merger. On the other hand it signalled the end of my close personal association with a business which, according to a quote given to Melvyn Marckus of the *Sunday Telegraph*, I had 'always nurtured, like a child'.

I suppose most people felt that I would retire to the country and put my feet up. This was never in my mind, but the shock of leaving when the following April came around was more than I had bargained for.

I lost my private office, my administrative back-up, my loyal staff and colleagues – but most of all my personal empire, bailiwick, call it what you will. For over thirty years I had been touring my sites, meeting my staff, taking my decisions, chatting with my guests and above all counting my successes. It had now gone.

I cannot tell you how empty my life felt when I realised that everything had come to an end. The fact that I was a wealthy man did not come into the equation: it was a sense of loss or even bereavement which had brought my world to what seemed to be such an abrupt conclusion.

Negative thoughts were never part of my business philosophy, but this experience had a devastating effect on my outlook on life. To make matters worse – the wound was self-inflicted. There were statements in the Press that the initiative for the Coral bid had come from me. This was not strictly the case.

I had been introduced to the company by Sidney Jenkins, a jobber whom I had known from my days in the City in the early 1920's. Sidney had his own firm, which was responsible for floating John Bairstow's Moat House Hotel group. He had good connections in the leisure industry and it was on his introduction that I commenced talks with Nicholas Coral.

Whatever my motives at the time, the fact is that I didn't have to make the sale. The company was in good shape. There just seemed to be some form of momentum taking over which I felt powerless to bring to an end. Perhaps I wanted someone to covet what was my own creation.

Quite apart from substantial interests in the holiday industry at home and overseas, I had taken Pontin's into solar energy after encouraging results from the use of panels in heating our swimming pools. I had also diversified into building and construction, when Ambrose Builders Limited was acquired in June 1977.

This company had been formed by Trevor Hemmings, who had been responsible for the major part of a £2.5 million contract to build our new holiday village in the sand dunes at Ainsdale, near Southport in 1968. He followed this a year or so later by similar work at Prestatyn on an even larger scale.

He had been a successful housebuilder and when the Southport contract neared completion, he sold this part of his business to Christian Salvesen for the sum of £1.7 million. Ambrose made an important contribution to group profits and Trevor became a large shareholder in Pontin's, having received 2,500,000 shares for his holding in the construction company.

It will be seen, therefore, that there was some justification for my view that a corporate acquisition of Pontin's would be an excellent investment for long term growth by any company wishing to become involved in an important sector of the leisure industry. Pontin's could be considered as having a degree of protection by the diversification into separate markets.

Another important factor was the fact that we had secured a more even cash flow as a result of the extended season, special events and the continued operation of centres in the Mediterranean.

Looking back, I feel sure that I was also being affected by a degree of frustration. Not only was there no logical and uncontroversial successor to be recruited from the ranks of my own board of management, but there had been a distinct lack of interest from what I would have called a bidder of some quality.

I knew that, despite the considerable efforts undertaken by the company's stockbrokers, our shares had never got near to attracting a triple "A" rating from the City. Financial journalists were never short of a story during the days of our rapid expansion, but had then written that Pontin's was a share that had failed to inspire investors.

When one becomes so closely identified with a successful enterprise, and is aware of the growth in value of the original investment, it is difficult to comprehend the attitude of the investing institutions. It appeared that, despite our profits record and sound asset-backing, Pontin's would never achieve the status of the so-called glamour stocks. We seemed destined to remain among the 'also-rans'.

We had our supporters, but in the City the holiday camp image would never lead to Pontin's becoming a 'Rolls-Royce' stock. Look what happened to them!

In the circumstances, Coral's genuine and enthusiastic interest was considered as a welcome development as far as I was concerned. When the final price was agreed I felt that, notwithstanding the reservations of our stockbrokers, Simon and Coates, I had obtained a good deal for our shareholders. This view was shared by the board, although there were some dissenting comments from members of my own family, as well as Ann Miller, once full details of the merger had been given to them.

Other than Sidney Jenkins, I had consulted no one about the very early stages of the Coral negotiations, not even Ann Miller, but I did take Bob Whitehead and Trevor Hemmings into my confidence once I was satisfied that a deal could be done. I asked them to join me at a meeting in my apartment at 55 Park Lane where they were introduced to Nicholas Coral, Michael Hoare and David Spencer, all members of the board of management of the Coral Group.

Bob and Trevor were sworn to secrecy. Once the price had been agreed it was, of course, necessary to inform the other members of the board and call in the professional advisers. It would be accurate to say that when I made the announcement at the meeting of the directors shock waves could be felt around the room. I know members of my family and Ann Miller could hardly believe what was happening.

A discussion took place during which it became clear that there was to be no unqualified support for the deal with Coral. Some members felt that an association with their gambling interests would not be good for the image of Pontin's. Ann Miller certainly made it clear that she felt that the merger would not be to the advantage of our company, and it was not too long before I started to share her thoughts. Very real doubts began to creep in and they never really left me.

Just a few days later, on 10 January, 1978, we had a further meeting of the directors to finalise certain matters to be included in the formal offer document. In addition to finalising a profit forecast, a most important element as far as the final price for the shares was concerned, there were other considerations: such as the company's rather generous non-contributory pension scheme and the possibility of the Office of Fair Trading becoming involved.

The minutes of this meeting clearly record that I was not satisfied with the terms of the deal, particularly as the value of Coral shares had fallen quite considerably since the terms were first announced. It was also clearly recorded that at that stage I was not prepared to be persuaded to declare my intentions in respect of the offer as far as my personal holding of nearly four million Pontin's shares were concerned.

It was stated at the meeting that my attitude was causing ill feeling at Coral, but this was to have no effect on the stance I was taking at that time.

It is interesting to record that these same minutes made it very clear that Trevor Hemmings and Bob Whitehead did not share my misgivings, the former going out of his way to reassure me and, presumably, everyone else present that all would be well and that the market in Coral shares would recover from the over-reaction to the merger of the two companies.

Bob Whitehead registered his concern that my attitude might have some adverse effect on the relationship with Coral. My second thoughts were, therefore, being resisted by colleagues on the board who were not members of my own family and close supporters.

Just ten days before the offer document was posted, a further meeting of the board was held and the minutes of this meeting clearly record that I commented on what I thought were omissions from the minutes of the previous meeting held eight days earlier. At *that* meeting I had continued to express my serious reservations on what was happening with the company.

A tape recording was played. After it had been heard by all concerned, Bob Whitehead felt it necessary to comment that, whether the directors liked it or not, Pontin's was being sold to another company and the new owners would be in ultimate control. He went on to say that we would not be able to do as we pleased, as had been the case in the past. These facts had to be accepted.

My misgivings were again discussed and the minutes record that Bob Whitehead, our Vice-Chairman, even commented on the fact that my letter to Pontin's shareholders seemed to be 'lacking in enthusiasm' for the deal. I was persuaded to think again on this point.

The momentum for the deal was undoubtedly there and my board was firmly enmeshed in the wealth of detail which accompany merger transactions of such magnitude. The combined group was to be capitalised at a figure in excess of £130 million, thus placing it in the forefront of the British leisure industry.

It was not a deal which could be easily cast aside, given that it was already a long way down the line and was receiving strong support from the non-family elements on the board.

It was significant that this latest meeting of the directors had not included the presence of my brother Harry, sister Elsie or Ann Miller. I was lacking in my usual personal support from these quarters. I was particularly upset that my old friend Jack Bishop, from whom I had acquired Seacroft Holiday Village at Hemsby-on-Sea in Norfolk some years previously, had sided with those who were enthusiastically supporting the Coral deal.

He later confided that he bitterly regretted that he had not seen that I was so very unhappy about the way matters were evolving.

Otherwise he may well have acted differently. He remarked that it would always be on his conscience but he knew that I had never sought fit to hold anything against him in this respect.

The time came for the final meeting at the Berkeley Square offices of Coral Leisure. Present were colleagues from Pontin's, representatives from the purchasers, merchant bankers, chartered accountants and solicitors. I confided my even more belated second thoughts to Percy Cansdale, whose firm had been auditors to the company for over thirty years.

I told him that I wanted to pull out of the deal, but he replied that matters had gone too far. If I did I would never again be able to show my face in the City.

Vice-Chairman Whitehead, who was a partner in solicitors Clifford Turner and Co., agreed with this view and said that everyone would be placed in an impossibly embarrassing position if I decided to withdraw from the deal.

By that time the board had recommended the deal to shareholders, had accepted in respect of their own shareholdings, and the investing institutions had done likewise. The papers were in their final form. Everyone felt that we had achieved a good price and the interests of the Pontin's shareholders would be best served if the takeover was completed in accordance with the agreed arrangements.

I had no option. Percy and Bob's advice was professionally sound and so, despite my deeply-held misgivings, the papers were signed and control of Pontin's passed to Coral Leisure. I know that Percy Cansdale feels that I have always resented the fact that I followed his recommendation and not my own judgement – however remiss – but this would be overstating the case.

Brother Harry died suddenly only a few weeks later and not long after the offer became unconditional. This fact has not left me with anything but sad memories of this particular period of my life. It has not been easy for me to provide this account of what was, after all is said and done, an ill-fated series of events as far as I was concerned.

Perhaps 'Thirteen' is an appropriate number for this unhappy chapter in my life . . .

I have already mentioned the Annual Reunions, which were always held in London and date back to the 1950's. At first these operated on a camp basis, with perhaps Little Canada or Pakefield having their own functions, but I soon recognised the value of getting everyone together, management, staff, regular guests, journalists and trade connections in the course of one spectacular night of entertainment each year.

This Gala Reunion was always billed as 'Pontin's Night of the Year' and in 1967 we graduated from the less glamorous Seymour or Porchester Halls to the Royal Albert Hall, where we made excellent use of the many boxes and licensed bars.

Various competitions were taking place at all of our sites during the season, such as the Miss Pontin Beauty Contest, Miss Max Factor, the amateur dancing events, donkey derbies, talent competitions, various indoor and outdoor sports and even the heats leading up to the Most Elegant Grandmother award. The prizes were always presented at the Royal Albert Hall and we also arranged for various celebrities to collect cheques on behalf of the charities which had been supported by guests at our sites.

There have been many well-known names over the years, but I recall visits from Dame Vera Lynn, Bob Monkhouse, Charlie Drake (an ex-Butlin's Redcoat), Bernard Bresslaw and the late Diana Dors, Dennis Price and Ben Lyon.

The evening's activities at every reunion were such that there was always something exciting taking place. The organisation was in the capable hands of David Lever, Pontin's Chief Entertainments Executive in association with Albert Stevenson, fellow member of the Grand Order of Water Rats and of the BBC.

My prime function was to act as host on these occasions. My private party always occupied the Royal Box, by special permission, and my very close friends had their own boxes on each side, so that I could pop in and out during the course of the evening.

Each Pontin's centre had its own licensed bar, each of which I visited during the evening. This is where the real reunions took place, with guests mixing with their special holiday friends and exchanging memories with the staff. Most of my clients met each other on just two occasions throughout the year: on their summer holidays and at the annual reunion.

Although being the host and having a high profile, I never ceased to be terrified of having to walk down the stairway on to the floor of the hall. There would be a fanfare of trumpets, the auditorium would be in darkness and the only illumination was the group of spotlights which were focused on my entrance.

The effect of this was to inflict virtually total blindness upon me. I was terrified of tripping head-over-heels, thus destroying the entire effect, but somehow I never did, though I would have been challenging the law of averages if the event had continued for many more years.

My speech was intended to tell everyone what was going on in the group by way of improvements and new attractions and put across my thanks to large numbers of my management and staff, to whom the annual reunion was the high spot of the year.

I knew that 1978, though, would be  my last as official host. I shall never forget the poignancy of the occasion. Fortunately it was not really appreciated at the time that it would be the last Pontin's spectacular at the Albert Hall, so matters did not become too emotional from that particular aspect.

But it does lead me to reflect that the decision to bring an end to the long sequence of annual reunions and gala occasions was linked to the loss of the 'family figurehead'. I trust no one will disillusion me in this respect, because that is the way in which I would like to feel the matter was handled by the new owners of what had, after all, been 'my' business for a period of over 30 years.

It was undoubtedly the end of an era. I left the scene with a heavy heart.

I cannot close this chapter without recalling just one more aspect of that last night at the Albert Hall. In my speech I paid tribute to Ann Miller and the enormous contribution which she had made to the success of Pontin's over a period of 30 years.

I disclosed to the audience that, although I was the one who was always upfront and took all the bows, she had been involved with every decision I had ever taken in the business, with the exception of one – the acceptance of terms from Coral.

I went on to say, with Nicholas Coral standing at my side, that I felt that not consulting her had been the biggest mistake of my life. Thousands of my loyal clients, members of staff, colleagues and close friends were listening to these remarks and I am told that Ann was in tears.

I suppose it could be said that April 1979 was the start of a fresh phase in my active life. I had an arrangement with Coral to  retain the flat at 55 Park Lane for a given period of time, so I made this the base for my future activities. I still retained the office premises in Pine Grange, Bournemouth, where Ann Miller continued to look after my affairs.

There was no question of retirement. It wasn't too long before I was talking to other people in the leisure industry.

*Chapter Fourteen*

# PRESIDENT FRED

BEFORE I finally relinquished my executive duties with Pontin's there was a very pleasant interlude.

One of my former entertainments' managers, Danny Bowshall had emigrated to Australia and settled down in Queensland, from where he had kept in touch. He persuaded me that there could be some attractive opportunities for setting up Potinental type holiday villages in one or two of the Eastern States.

Arrangements were made for me to pay a visit Down Under, so, in February 1979, I left with a very full itinerary taking in a visit to Singapore on the outward journey and a stopover in Hong Kong on the return flight.

Danny had carried out some useful preparatory work and he made arrangements for me to meet the premiers of Queensland and New South Wales, who expressed a great deal of willingness and enthusiasm for my type of leisure project. They offered incentives, such as a grant-aid and low interest bearing loans, which would have left Pontin's with all of the equity.

They were very keen to promote tourism on the Gold Coast, with a view to attracting visitors from Japan, Malaysia and Hong Kong, and felt that Pontinental-style villages would be ideal for this purpose.

I attended civic receptions, and I was interviewed on TV and radio, as well as by the Press. All-in-all I was very impressed with the prospect of yet another sphere of operations.

A twin series of Test Matches was just coming to an end, Australia being host to both England and the West Indies after the

resumption of 'peace' in the cricket world following the dispute
with Kerry Packer's World Series cricket camp. Australia were in
the process of achieving a clean sweep in the series against
England, thus regaining the Ashes following England's five wins to
one defeat on home ground in 1977, but all was not doom and
gloom.

I remember attending a very lively birthday party for Fred
Trueman, at which I was fortunate enough to meet some of the
best-known names in post-war cricket, as well as the famous 'Fiery
Fred': Richie Benaud, Sir Gary Sobers, who was knighted in 1975,
and England and Essex cricketer of considerable distinction, Trevor
'Barnacle Bill' Bailey, who was also a star performer for
Walthamstow Avenue's post-war football team.

I gained access to this rather select celebration because I had met
Trevor and his wife, Greta, while flying out to Australia. I was
travelling first-class and could find no one interesting to talk to, so
I carried out a recce towards the rear of the aircraft and came
across Trevor and Greta, together with two of their friends, Frank
and Celia Wilson. I rather attached myself to them and we had
some excellent times together both in Australia and on the return
journey.

Whilst I was carrying out my business activities, Trevor and
Greta moved on to Tasmania to visit friends and Frank and Celia
carried out a similar mission in New Zealand. We all agreed to
meet again in Sydney for the Test Match before flying home via
Hong Kong, where we spent three nights and enjoyed some
wonderful meals.

I was very excited at what proved to be my only opportunity to
see test cricket at such a famous venue as Sydney, and my new
friends used their influence by arranging for me to join them in the
members' stand.

I had purchased a movie camera the day before so I could record
some highlights of this fight for the Ashes. With this in mind I
moved down to the front row of the stand which had been taken
over by the Press photographers. These hard-nosed Antipodeans
did not make things too easy for me, but I managed to shoot some
footage of the players leaving the pavilion as well as some of the
action on the field of play

I have no record of this important sporting occasion though . . .
I left the lens cap on the camera! This caused me much
embarrassment and frustration but Celia Wilson still recalls the

episode with considerable merriment because I provided everyone with a very good laugh.

In the course of our return stopover in Hong Kong I remember visiting a shop where Frank bought Celia a most magnificent handbag. I felt that I wanted to repay some of the kindness which had been shown to me on that memorable trip, so I decided to purchase an identical item for Greta Bailey. I am not sure whether or not it would have been her own choice of accessory, but, at least, it provided her with a memento of what was undoubtedly a pleasant trip, and which had afforded me a measure of escape from my stresses in the UK.

The stresses were soon there again. Within only a few weeks of my return I found myself bidding farewell to my personal staff and having to re-arrange my business life. Any investment in Australia was forgotten.

Take it from me that it was a strange and considerably unnerving experience to find myself with the proverbial empty in-tray after many years of continual and sometimes frenzied activity, it was almost like being in outer space.

To pursue this analogy even further, the camps, villages and holiday centres were literally on another planet so far as I was concerned. Whatever was happening in the world of Pontin's, one factor was for sure – they had no further need for my guiding hand.

If decisions needed to be made – there was someone else to make them.

Negative thinking has never been part of my make-up or temperament however. The immediate task was to find myself something to do. This could mean only one thing: I needed another business. Not one to be started from scratch but perhaps some promising enterprise which could benefit from my rich vein of experience in the leisure industry.

I had a number of exploratory meetings with a number of leisure industry tycoons, but I could never come to the right sort of agreement and formula where I could really commit myself.

I continued to look around for other propositions. I was amused to find that my birthday on 24 October is shared by broadcaster Sir Robin Day and Rolling Stone Bill Wyman, but the star sign of Scorpio appears to be the only thing we have in common. It may well be, as the *Evening Standard* put it in an article in October 1979, that they have shared Fred Pontin's special talent of putting into effect a unique formula of combining business with pleasure.

I applied this philosophy when I invested £300,000 in purchasing a thatched hotel-pub-restaurant known as The Fisherman's Cot situated in a well-known beauty spot on the banks of the River Exe, near Tiverton in Devon.

There were only fourteen bedrooms, but there was planning permission for a further 23 chalet-style bedrooms at this favourite retreat for anglers wishing to enjoy the fine salmon and trout fishing in the area.

Sister Elsie was living not too far away at Stoke Gabriel, near Totnes, and she agreed to help me in supervising the new business. This was my second hotel. I had owned the Farringford Hotel at Freshwater since 1968, when I purchased it for the second time, having bought and sold it eight years previously.

Farringford – former home of Alfred, Lord Tennyson – occupies a superb site with a swimming pool, croquet lawn, tennis courts and a nine-hole golf course designed by Clive Clark. I still make very regular visits to the hotel and enjoy entertaining my friends and close colleagues there, especially at Christmas.

This hotel featured in one or two 'paper' transactions in the Eighties, but I have never relinquished an interest in a property I regard with a great deal of affection for a number of reasons.

My most successful racehorse, Specify, spent the last of his days at Farringford, of course, and I also remember the frequent visits of Lord Mountbatten when he was Governor of the Isle of Wight. He would make a habit of calling in for morning coffee or afternoon tea and I got to know him quite well.

I once stayed at his home and drove him up to London the next morning in my much-cherished Bentley. He also visited my holiday camp at Little Canada – as part of his official duties, not as a paying customer!

I recall that in the year of his assassination by the I.R.A. I had asked him if he would able to be present at a charitable function with which I was involved. He explained that he had to decline the invitation because each July was reserved for a family holiday in Galway on the West Coast of Ireland.

When I remarked upon the security aspects of such a sensitive visit, he dismissed the risks by saying that he was 'very well known locally', had been going there for many years, and 'always enjoyed the company of the people of Galway'. He never returned from his visit in that particular year. His brutal death shocked the whole of the civilised world.

Because of the Farringford connection with Lord Louis, a local resident, Mrs Gertrude Gilchrist, ably assisted by Ann Miller, organised a floral festival at the hotel as a tribute to the dead hero. The premises were taken over by superb displays of flowers provided by members of local flower clubs. The arrangements reflected the national colours of countries in which Lord Mountbatten had served during his long and distinguished career.

Pontin's was never far from my mind, however in the months that followed my departure from the Coral Group. During 1979 I had kept in touch with what had been going on, even ringing up some of my former managers, who were undoubtedly suffering from split loyalties as a result of the takeover. Towards the end of that particular year I had let it be known that I was very much in the hunt to buy back my former company from Coral.

People have said that I was smiling, because of Coral's difficulties, but I was genuinely concerned. I could see that the parent company could be in serious trouble in terms of cash flow and the adverse effect on their borrowing ratios if they lost their casino gaming licences.

I wanted them to know that I was a very interested party. Unfortunately there were some very big guns on the battlefield. I had no real chance of matching the bid which eventually came from Bass. Grand Metropolitan had been on the scene a little earlier, the negotiations having been conducted by Maxwell Joseph and Michael Hoare at a figure of 106p for each Coral share.

There was, however, the problem of a reference to the Monopolies and Mergers Commission, which ruled that Grand Met would not be permitted to buy Centre Hotels, which were in Coral's ownership.

Grand Met subsequently withdrew and Bass came to the forefront, having already been engaged in negotiations with Trevor Hemmings, who was representing Coral. Bass's earlier offers had been rejected by the Coral board, but when they came back at the same level as Grand Met's figure in a more favourable market – and also added a dividend – the deal was done.

It will be appreciated that the management and staff of Pontin's had now entered yet another period of uncertainty, having been bought and sold twice in a comparatively short time scale.

Although the Pontinental business had continued under Coral's ownership, Peter Hopper resigned from the board of Coral Leisure because an ex-director of EMI Leisure and Mecca, Peter Delaney

Smith, had been brought in over his head towards the end of 1979.

This, alongside other circumstances, had triggered my own premature departure from the Coral Group.

I was very anxious to explore the possibility of renewing my association with my former business as a means of providing a stabilising factor. Derek Palmer of Bass did not respond favourably, however, to my approaches in this respect. I had in mind the position of President of Pontin's, but there was no support for such an idea amongst the decision-takers at Bass.

By early 1980 I came to accept the fact that Pontin's could no longer be of any concern of mine. I witnessed from afar the eventual sale of the Pontinental side of the business, with the exception of Pineta Beach, Sardinia. I concluded that Bass had no regard for the group as a holiday and leisure business, and took no real interest in what I had created in those post-war years.

To them it seemed to be just a 'free house' with enormous sales. They never demonstrated to me any real understanding of the industry in general or Pontin's in particular.

There were changes in the location of office premises, involving a move within Bournemouth and then on to Banbury in Oxfordshire, which resulted in many staff leaving the company. There had also been a succession of Bass-appointed chairmen and directors. Mike Austin left the company in 1984, as did Graham Parr and one or two other leading executives who had been trained under my leadership and who I would have described as key players.

Mike Austin, who had a two year running consultancy with Bass, also kept in touch with what was going on through Trevor Hemmings, but the latter also decided to leave in June 1985. I understand that at that time he had talked about a possible buy-out with Peter Williams, the chairman at Pontin's, who was also in charge of Crest Hotels, another part of the Bass group of leisure interests.

This never came to anything. According to Trevor, such a sale would have resulted in the need for a Class 4 circular under the rules applicable to a public company, and disclosure of price and current profitability at Pontin's might well have caused questions from Bass shareholders.

Trevor Hemmings returned to some of his outside interests and became engaged in new enterprises, but he never allowed his fascination for Pontin's to fall by the wayside. He could see that it might well be only a question of time before he would have another opportunity to get back into the frame.

He also knew that I was also prepared to respond to any call to get under starter's orders again. Trevor paid me the compliment in 1986 of letting me know his intentions, so I could perhaps be forgiven for concluding that he wanted me to be part of the deal. There was, alas, no clear-cut line of demarcation and my own overtures to Bass were getting back to Trevor, who was really engaged upon doing his own thing.

I had brought close colleague and 'company doctor' Ronnie Aitken into the picture, and there were meetings with Trevor on the subject of funding a buy-out, but he concluded the deal on his own and I was not successful in negotiating any part of the transaction for my particular corner.

As Trevor described the situation only recently, I had been placed in a 'suspense account'. In other words, some form of 'reserve' or perhaps 'contingency arrangement', which, in the event, was never required.

The sums involved were enormous. The final figure was £57 million, excluding Pontinental because the offer fell short of what Bass was seeking. Swallowing all of my considerable pride, I have to concede that Trevor Hemmings proved that he was fully capable of arranging the complicated structure which was required to finance the acquisition.

Virtually the entire amount was borrowed and supported by the personal assets of all concerned.

Trevor had identified the people who were to make up his managerial team. The fact that all had been trained by me was really irrelevant – they could not be in both camps and Trevor had established that the banks were not looking upon my presence as an essential requirement for completing the transaction.

Every dog has his day. I now know that my age was against me, and that the business had moved on in the seven years since I had left the fold.

Trevor Hemmings had become enmeshed in the world of 'mezzanine finance', 'zero coupons', and 'deep-discounted bonds' . . . a far cry from what I had been used to. It was a bitter pill to swallow, but I have not allowed this further disappointment to deter me from further forays in the business which had been my life for forty years.

I was not aware at the time of the true nature of the interest of Scottish & Newcastle Breweries in Trevor Hemmings' negotiations with Bass. I have since learned that they were given what amounted to a 'call option' on the shares in Pontin's. I was under the impression that they were in the background on some form of financial basis connected with the opportunity which would be afforded in terms of supplying the sites, but they were, in effect, acting as some form of security back-up, providing comfort to the financial backers.

Given that Scottish & Newcastle have now exercised their option in two equal stages, thus achieving 100% control of Pontin's, the confidence demonstrated by Trevor's bankers can be clearly understood. This deal undoubtedly put Scottish & Newcastle also beyond the reach of Elders at the time they were seeking to acquire control of the group by virtue of their hostile bid.

Profitability assumed far better proportions once Bass had relinquished the business. Scottish & Newcastle had providentially decided to accelerate the exercise of their options, because to have delayed for too long could have cost them an even higher price.

The division of Scottish and Newcastle which includes Holiday Club Pontin's and Center Parcs can now offer 18 million bed-nights per annum. I see no reason why I should not make the point that this massive business has grown from the foundation stone of Leslie Dean's former wartime site at Brean Sands. This division accounts for *one-third* of the aggregate profits of the parent company.

The morning after the deal had been completed, and Pontin's was under his control, Trevor Hemmings called at my apartment in Whitehall Court and offered me the position of Founder President of what has now become known as Holiday Club Pontin's.

He told me that it was the unaminous decision of all concerned and it was intended as an acknowledgement of a lifetime's work.

I was more than happy to accept, and, despite any misgivings which may been entertained by Trevor and his team, there has never been any question of my interfering with the way they run the business, which I am convinced is in very good hands.

I am flattered that my portrait still hangs in the boardroom in the new centralised office premises in Chorley, Lancashire, and perhaps, just perhaps, a glance from time to time at the expression on my face may well influence or even inspire them in their deliberations.

'Now what would Sir Fred have done?' Am I being unduly egoistic? Probably. Yet that's what they would all expect – and who am I to let them down?

It is comforting for me to know that Holiday Club Pontin's is now controlled by people who were brought into the business by me. We had a lot of fun working together and I was gratified to learn that they have applied the Pontin's business acumen and managerial expertise in re-organising a totally diverse business.

Langdale, the site which I had introduced to Trevor Hemmings some years previously, is now a four-star luxury Time Share development in the Lake District. Formerly a caravan site, it is part of the Scottish & Newcastle group and Pontin's were called in to sort out a few problems.

Mike Austin tells me that the up-market owners suffered what amounted to a total culture shock when they heard that Pontin's were moving in, but now they agree that it has never been run so efficiently.

Well done the lads!

Following the acquisition of The Fisherman's Cot, I was interested in making similar purchases in the West Country. I purchased the Palomino Pony Inn in Honiton, followed in 1983 by the Berry Head Hotel in Brixham, which commanded superb views across Torbay.

It was like old times to be back in Brixham applying for a licence from the local magistrates. I had last seen them when I acquired the Dolphin and St Mary's Bay Holiday Villages and the Wall Park Holiday Centre for Pontin's way back in 1961.

Elsie was again involved with supervising these latest purchases, and I set about the task of improving the facilities and services on the basis of my long-standing maxim of providing value for money. By the time I had completed my small group of hotels I had also added The Trout Inn, on the waterside and just across the road from The Fisherman's Cot.

All this had to come to an end after a few years when Elsie reached her seventieth birthday and her husband Bob was seventy-three. They felt that they had earned retirement. Regular visits to all four sites was becoming too much of an effort for them.

Quite apart from supervision, they handled the book-keeping, purchasing and VAT returns and there were always some problems requiring attention, especially those relating to staff. It had to be faced, too, that the properties needed continual capital investment to keep them up to modern standards.

This was the overall deciding factor to sell. I was a reluctant seller, but I realised that I could not expect the West Country branch of my family to carry on for ever. I sold all four units during 1986 and 1987 and reflected once again on my ill-fortune in not having my long-sought-after family succession firmly in place.

Before these sales were effected, however, another public company proposition had attracted my interest. Ronnie Aitken, wearing his company doctor hat, had been drafted into a fast-failing rag trade company known as Kunick Holdings. He quickly recognised that he was dealing with a hopeless case, but saw the potential in treating the company as a 'shell'. It could be brought back to life if the necessary assets and entrepreneurial expertise were introduced, with the ultimate blessing of the Stock Exchange. He agreed a moratorium with creditors and set about a re-construction of the company.

The newspapers decided that my activities were still of some interest to their readers, apparently because *of* rather than *despite* my advancing years. 'Next on 76-year old Sir Fred's menu?' 'Yet another come-back by Sir Fred Pontin.' 'Sir Fred, a real stayer.' Quotes from the national press in May 1983 when the Kunick deal was announced.

I had been brought in with Don Robinson, a charming and most successful businessman from Yorkshire, who also chaired Hull City football club. He had sold Scarborough Zoo to Trident Television in 1973, but had retained his interest in leisure by his ownership of Scarborough Opera House, a showboat pub and a half stake in two discos. He injected these assets into Kunick for £138,000 cash and six million new shares.

I contributed the Farringford Hotel in exchange for £200,000 in cash, plus three million new 10p shares at par, which I subsequently placed with institutions at a 50% profit.

Kunick had now become a leisure company, but it was to be some years before a quotation on the Unlisted Securities Market, and ultimately a full listing, was to be achieved.

Other deals were to follow later that year. In August, Don Robinson arranged to buy back Scarborough Zoo and Marineland Amusement Park from Trident Television. He introduced these additional cash producing assets into the re-named Kunick Leisure in exchange for more new shares, which gave Trident a 21.5% stake in Kunick.

In the meantime I was concentrating my efforts on persuading Annabel Geddes to part with her ghoulish exhibition of torture, disease and violent death known as the London Dungeon, which she had turned into one of London's top tourist attractions.

Located under railway arches near London Bridge, this business was producing annual profits of £200,000 on a turnover of only three times this figure. It was my view that the actual returns could be far higher, given improved controls and a more disciplined approach to book-keeping. I was soon proved correct.

The negotiations were quite protracted and accompanied by the consumption of considerable quantities of champagne, but we got there in the end. The purchase price was a mixture of cash and shares amounting to £1 million.

I also did well out of this deal. I took three million of the Kunick shares which were allocated to Annabel by paying her the par value of 10p for each share in cash. In other words, I underwrote the issue to a certain extent, thus smoothing the way to a satisfactory completion.

I eventually disposed of these shares at a very useful profit . . . so the London Dungeon has never held any horrors as far as I am concerned!

The Dungeon deal again hit the headlines with headlines such as: 'Pontin's buy is quite a scream' and 'From holidays to horror'. This publicity served to increase the takings at the turnstiles. As a result it was not long before this new investment made a significant contribution to Kunick's overall profit performance and the market price of the shares.

I stayed with Kunick Leisure for four years and left on a perfectly amicable basis. I also made a hefty profit on the disposal of my shares.

Another useful spin-off for me was that I inherited Leon Andrews from the management. He has been a close associate of mine ever since, and I have come to value his friendship and loyal support. He is secretary and director of most of my private companies and it is comforting for me to know that they are in such good administrative hands.

*Chapter Fifteen*

# 'NATIONAL ASSET'

MANY REASONS are given by people in various walks of life for writing their autobiography or reminiscences. I cannot pretend to have any particular or exclusive explanation for my own efforts in this regard.

I have come to appreciate that an inevitable adjunct to the whole exercise is a tendency to reflect upon the following . . . Why did it happen? How did it all come about? How have I played my role? What have I achieved? Perhaps for the first time in my life give some consideration as to how I have seen myself. Speculate upon how others may have passed judgement on me.

I have always been aware that I was very fortunate to have been given an extraordinary supply of energy. This was a significant contributory factor in helping me fulfil my very early ambitions to make a lot of money.

I found there was no set path. No signposts to be followed. No sources of advice to be heeded above all others. I simply proceeded along my own route, took my chances, which were mainly based upon my own judgement, and mastered my own destiny.

If asked if I would have done certain things in another way I would reply that if I had I would have been a 'different person' – so the question does not really arise.

Some of my closest friends have described my character as 'enigmatic'. I cannot accept this description in the truest sense of the word. There are times when my conduct may have been considered to be unpredictable, but I feel that most people have known where they stood with me. In the final outcome they would have been aware that I have usually tried to be fair in dealing with the multitude of situations confronting me over the years.

My staff and colleagues became accustomed to the sudden explosion of anger, the invective and the barely controlled irritation at what I invariably recognised as incompetence. Unless I was dealing with something totally unacceptable, my display of what many would have regarded as 'petulance' – but which I considered to be an essential weapon of discipline – would be followed by the velvet glove. Perhaps represented by a hand on the shoulder and a drink at the bar.

Anyone at the sharp end of this type of performance knew that, more often than not, it was an ephemeral feature of my conduct. I did not tend to harbour any long term grudges.

On the basis that I am treating my 'not guilty' plea to the charge of being an enigma as sustained, perhaps I should comment upon some of the evidence which has been provided in support of the allegations.

My public image is said to differ widely from how my close friends and associates have come to accept me. I put this down to one particularly important factor. If my staff have regarded me as some form of autocrat, it is probably because they have been severely criticised by their Chairman and asked to do something which they may have regarded as unnecessary or . irrelevant.

They would have experienced the sharp edge of my tongue – but then be faced with that pat. It may have been conduct of a rather ambiguous or even bewildering nature, yet it got results.

Sister Elsie has always said that my greatest strengths were a determination to succeed and an ability to get people to do exactly what I wanted. Staff came to appreciate this style of management. Not always, though, before they had found it necessary to pour out their hearts to whoever happened to be near at hand, usually someone like Ann Miller, who must have been responsible for suppressing many a letter of resignation in her day.

Whatever other people may have thought about this style of management, it was important that I was confident that it worked. It produced the required results.

It has been said that these methods would sometimes lead to me getting the wrong answers to important questions. Answers which were given out of fear, rather than frankness and sincerity. This may well have been the case, but I could usually tell the 'yes men' from those who would stand their ground and argue their case. The survivors soon learned to do this and they were usually rewarded with promotion and increased responsibilities.

To continue with this theme, Ann Miller reflects that she has seen me 'wipe the floor with a person', but 'he or she would still come back for more'. Perhaps it was because some of the staff never really knew how I was likely to respond to a given situation, and this generated some perverse form of loyalty. Born, perhaps, out of the challenge of survival.

In writing a personal account of my experiences I suppose it will be expected that an uninhibited account of my private life should enter the debate. There will be disappointment here. I am very much of the opinion that a line has to be drawn if one is to respect the privacy and intimate feelings of some of the people who have been close to me over the years.

My wife Dorothy has been tolerant, understanding, loving and even forgiving in respect of my admitted tendency to philander over many years. We were married in 1929, and it must be said that these six decades or so have not been easy for her, especially now that she suffers from arthritis.

She had made it clear that she thought I was mad to get involved with holiday camps in the first place and she has admitted that she found the rapid rate of expansion totally incomprehensible. She realised that if confidence was required to succeed I would not be lacking in this department and from the early days she played her part in the family business.

She did this despite the fact that my constant travelling and socialising precluded even the slimmest chances of establishing a normal family relationship. According to Dorothy, our daughter Pat was not even aware she had a father until she had grown up. I very much hope that this is an exaggeration, but there must be some truth in it.

Although we continue to live independent lives, Dorothy and I see each other virtually every weekend. There have been quite a few family homes over the years, but she now lives in Cranbrook, Kent surrounded by lovely countryside in a wing of a house which belongs to my daughter and son-in-law. During the week I am usually in my apartment in London, and these regular weekend visits to Dorothy would be sorely missed if they ever came to an end.

Whatever interpretation is advanced for the exact nature of my relationship with Dorothy, my marriage could well be described as the sheet anchor of my life and no one is likely to be able to persuade me otherwise.

Those who know me are aware that I have never lacked the company of an attractive woman when I needed an escort on numerous social and other occasions. Dorothy says she never took to the sort of social life I was leading when my business was expanding. I worked very hard, but I also knew how to relax.

I enjoyed the company of others, and this gregariousness extended to just about everything which Dorothy found unappealing. I was to be found in boxing halls, expensive hotels, racecourses, football grounds, private clubs and smart restaurants. I thrived on it.

My charitable activities necessitated attendance at a myriad of functions, and, as far as business was concerned, it was important to be in a position to entertain important people at very short notice.

I have been fortunate enough to have been surrounded by people whom I came to trust and whose opinions I have respected. I have also enjoyed the loyal support of a devoted family, who became closely identified with the success of my career in the holiday camp industry. They could never be described as 'fellow travellers', because they worked just as hard as I did.

Leslie Dean, the original owner of Brean Sands and Osmington Bay, remained a director and shareholder for some years, but left after a disagreeement on policy during the 1950s. I have remained in fairly regular contact, however, with the Dean family

The family retained connections with the holiday camp business at Southdean, Middleton-on-Sea, near Bognor Regis on a site purchased from Mr & Mrs Shaw-Porter on the insistence of Leslie's daughter, Valerie. Valerie was keen to become involved in the industry, having previously worked for me at Brean Sands. Leslie died in 1970; his widow Audrey is still living at Middleton, as is Auntie Vi, the widow of Arthur James, who was my first manager at Brean Sands

Valerie Barnett (née Dean), who opened the front door of 'Fairfield' to me back in 1946, now runs the very attractive and popular Mill Hotel at Kingham, Oxfordshire, where she and husband John have built up a successful business with a fine reputation.

Leslie Dean was an enthusiastic cricketer, whose play was of county standard. He was so keen that he even arranged for Audrey to travel to London for the birth of their first child, just in case it was a boy and so that he could qualify to play for Surrey.

In the event they had daughter Valerie, but brother Brian followed within a year or so, although his preference has been for tennis rather than his father's beloved game of cricket.

In putting this story on record, I have come to appreciate the extent to which I have influenced the lives of others in what must now be seen as a remarkable manner. This rather belated realisation has had a somewhat chastening effect upon me, but my success has also been theirs.

I am not conscious of too many regrets being harboured along the way, except perhaps some very personal misgivings from Ann Miller and my wife.

I am by no means a religious man, but I understand that it was St Paul who wrote, admittedly in another context, that: 'I am what I am'. The common use of this expression has assuredly served as a form of justification for the equivocal actions of many men in similar circumstances, but this is not a justifiable excuse by any means.

Reflecting on what I shall be leaving behind when I eventually depart from this world, Pontin's could perhaps be described as a memorial to its founder. But what of my family? Peter Hopper married my daughter Patricia in 1960, but he never demonstrated any real enthusiasm at the time for the holiday camps in England and Wales, although he did spend some time involved with the management of the newly acquired Little Canada Holiday Village on the Isle of Wight.

My wife and daughter worked there for some time in the early days and Peter was in the habit of travelling down to see Patricia at most weekends. They had earlier met when both were on the same catering course at the London Bakery School at Borough Polytechnic and before Peter joined his family's bread baking and retailing business in Kent.

When he sought my permission to marry Pat I saw this as an opportunity to introduce him to the holiday camp business. I was, quite naturally, having thoughts about succession. I even went as far as to make it a condition of my approval of the marriage, but Peter soon sought a release from this undertaking so he could take up an offer from Hovis McDougall to manage a factory they had built following the acquisition of the Hopper family's baking business.

Within two years Hovis McDougalls had been taken over by Rank and Peter rejoined Pontin's where he became very much involved with Pontinental.

Pat and Peter are now established on their farm at Cranbrook. They have a total of almost 180 acres of land and a flourishing farm shop. They fatten chickens, pigs and bullocks as well as produce lambs.

They have thousands of fruit trees, as befits the Garden of England and I know that Pat has never been happier. She works as hard as I ever did and enjoys every minute of it. I love keeping up to date with life down on the farm during my regular weekend visits. I am very proud of her achievements.

Their four children, all boys, were educated at Kings, Canterbury and have been well looked after by a trust I created many years ago. I am told that the aggregate capital value now exceeds £1½ million. The word PINK is how I remember their names: Paul, Ian, Neil and Kevin. Two of them are involved with the farm and the shop, one as catering manager and the other in all manner of enterprises.

What a pity they could not be persuaded to enter my business, but I am afraid that they received no encouragement from their parents, especially their father, who wouldn't even let them work at the holiday camps during their summer holidays. I felt that they might conceivably savour the atmosphere of the sites, become interested in the business, and possibly choose a career with the company. However, I was not successful with my little ploy.

Sister Elsie and husband Bob are now enjoying a well-earned retirement at their lovely home in Devon. Brother Len and his wife Hilda are also retired and living nearby. They spend most of their time gardening and playing bowls, rather successfully in both activities.

Stan Butt, formerly the manager of a butcher's shop in Bristol, who once sold his employer's wares to the labour camp I ran at Bedminster, became a major supplier of meat and related products to all of my units in the West of England. He could be said to have enjoyed the material benefits derived from a large turnover.

I was instrumental in encouraging him in what must have been one of the earliest management buy-outs, when he was uncertain as to whether or not he should buy the business from its owner. The asking price was £15,000, but I recommended that he should bid £10,000, payable over a period of three years from profits. I also told Stan to inform his boss that if these terms were not agreed, Fred Pontin's business would be lost to the firm. He did the deal on this basis – and never looked back.

Many other people have benefited: lawyers, accountants, breweries, wine and spirit merchants and other suppliers, and, of course, H. M. Collector of Taxes.

Throughout my life I have represented myself as just an ordinary man who has never sought to lose the common touch. This has been despite a long standing exposure to a way of life which has brought me into contact with some of the leading figures in many strata of British society.

*Thumbs Up!* seems to be particularly appropriate, bearing in mind the television advertisement which showed me doing just this when extolling the virtues of booking early back in the 1970's.

I arrived at the studios in late afternoon, not long before the director intended calling a halt to the day's proceedings in which they were preparing the final version of our latest television campaign. I had a look at what had been produced and decided that my own presence in the short advertising clip would be a positive improvement. Leslie Crowther was at the studio, and, being a fellow Barker in the Variety Club, he readily responded to my request that he should make some form of introduction to my appearance on the advertisement.

I have to say that the director did not take too kindly to my intervention. As I was the boss he had little say in the matter. What had not been decided, however, was what I should be doing on film.

Mike Austin had an answer: 'For heaven's sake, just look into the camera, smile and say 'Book Early'. What could be more simple?'

It would have been easy for a professional, but it took quite a few takes before everyone was satisfied. Sometimes I got the smile right, but had my thumb coming up too late. Other times there was a rapid thumb movement but only a sickly smile.

All was well in the end. Those few seconds on the Pontin's TV advertisement brought us more publicity and attention – not to mention increased bookings – than anything else, which might have cost hundreds of thousands of pounds. Corny maybe – but it worked. That's all that counts when it comes to marketing a good product.

There is no particular moral to my life story, even though Lewis Caroll wrote in *Alice in Wonderland*: 'Everthing's got a moral if you can only find it.' I have already confessed to having no religious beliefs, so if there is any Guiding Light it can perhaps be attributed only to a sense of being aware of and, on occasions, caring for the feelings, sensibilities and unfortunate circumstances of others.

Hence my strong inclination towards support for charitable causes.

Over the years I have established probably an over-exaggerated reputation for helping any member of my staff or any special friend if I considered my assistance was necessary, if it was deserved and hopefully would be appreciated.

I say this because many odd stories have somehow found their way back to me under this particular heading and I would have to be some sort of saint for them all to have been true.

It is correct that I have always had what could be described as an obsessional hatred of illness in any form, and I suppose any generosity I may have shown was probably linked to a need to purge the obsession by trying to assist in removing its cause.

I remember helping out Walter Rowley, for example, when his first wife became seriously ill in Majorca. The local medical facilities seemed incapable of coping with what proved to be a haemorrhage of the brain so I flew out to arrange for her immediate repatriation to England for treatment at the London Hospital, where I had excellent connections.

She survived no less than three serious operations and lived for a further six years, which gave us all a great deal of satisfaction.

Walter's wife was a very special person to me, but there have been other instances when I have been happy to be of assistance, where it was thought necessary to short-circuit the National Health Service to set certain minds at rest.

A business can only be successful if the management and staff are not distracted by extraneous circumstances and illness of a loved one can certainly come under this heading.

Tim Moorcroft, a member of my managerial team, became ill with cancer at a crucial time in his career. Being a director on the main board it was entirely justified that he should receive the best possible attention, but I like to think that, given similar circumstances, other valued members of the staff received the same consideration.

There was an occasion when I appreciated at first hand what care from others in moments of distress can mean. This was when I was involved in a serious motor car accident late at night in 1957.

The car I was driving was in collision with a trolley bus stanchion in Billet Road, Walthamstow. It happened to be Ann Miller's new car, a Ford Consul which I had picked up that particular day, my Bentley being in for a service.

It would appear that I had fallen asleep at the wheel of the vehicle and the crash caused me to lose consciousness. It was very fortunate that the sound of the impact attracted the attention of a young mother who was attending to the needs of her baby. She had the presence of mind to call an ambulance and other emergency services.

There were no compulsory seatbelts in those days and I suffered fractures to my sternum and every rib in my body, in addition to a punctured lung, which caused internal bleeding. It took two hours to release me from the wrecked car and get me to the casualty unit at Whipp's Cross Hospital. I transferred to the London Hospital early on the following day.

I learned much later that the disturbed journey over so many eneven cobblestones to Whipp's Cross probably saved my life – I coughed up the blood, which was dispersed rather than being retained in such a vulnerable organ of my body.

I must have looked as if I was on my way out. When I arrived at the casualty department I was asked for details of my religion. I have never had any religious belief and probably replied 'atheist', but there must have been some form of guardian angel watching over me.

That young mother who had demonstrated such commendable alertness, but whom I can now only recall as Mrs Smith, undoubtedly saved my life. It was with a great deal of pleasure that for many years after I was able to show my appreciation by arranging for her and her family to have their choice of regular annual holidays as well as a packed Christmas hamper.

An incident such as this demonstrates just how significant a part luck and good fortune have played in my life, so it is little wonder that I can be affected by the misfortune of others.

I needed an extended period of convalescence after the accident, during which time Dickie Doyle took over as acting chairman.

I justify my attitude to religion, to a certain extent, in the knowledge that most wars are born out the intolerance of other people's religious beliefs.

I recognise that much has been said and written about the existence of a Supreme Being. Cardinal Newman ventured the opinion that there were only two supreme and luminously self-evident beings: 'Myself and my Creator.' I would not argue too much with that when the dominant influence in my life has been my own personality. I am without an acknowledged faith, however, and I know that this has been a source of distress to some of the people who have figured prominently in my life.

I have achieved just about everything I really wanted. There have been disappointments, but these have been almost exclusively associated with the deeds of others, especially where I felt that my trust had been betrayed.

Many people have set out in ways very similar to my own, but the order of life is such that not all can succeed. It is inevitable that failure should be experienced by some in order that success can be achieved by others. This book has been an attempt to illustrate that if doors open it is usually for a purpose. You can decide either to go through . . . or you turn and walk away. I never hesitated in passing into whatever happened to lie within. I was seldom disappointed.

If I was, another door usually appeared before too long and I soon learned that it did not pay to look back. That would have been a negative reaction.

I always sought to benefit from a previous experience then press on to the next opportunity. I recommend this philosophy to anyone really prepared to grab what life has to offer.

I have enjoyed good and robust health for most of my entire life, but I was certainly hit for six a few years ago when I discovered that I had cancer. I thought I knew all about hospitals after my car accident, but this was a totally different experience. I could not be certain whether I would survive, and if I did, what would be the quality of the remainder of my life.

Cancer of the stomach and bowel was diagnosed after I had been experiencing severe abdominal pains. The operation involved the removal of large areas of both organs and a colostomy, which was undertaken in a highly skilled manner.

I had always hated any thought of illness, whether in myself or in others. I did not react in the most positive of manners when I was released from the London Clinic. Part of my convalescence was spent with Elsie and Bob at their home in Stoke Gabriel, where I was by no means an ideal patient, feeling very wretched and miserable at the thought of the indignity of it all.

My sister did all she could to inspire me to look on the bright side. She reminded me that I could have been looking out at a brick wall in the back streets of London rather than at her very attractive millpond and wildlife.

Many people will be aware of what is involved as a result of a colostomy and Elsie helped me to deal with my psychological hang-up. She encouraged me to accept the condition I was in. She further reminded me that other public figures had gone through the same operation, yet still carried on once the routine had been accepted. Elsie helped me adapt to a more disciplined way of life and, providing I am careful about when and what I eat and drink, I can cope with the inevitable limitations in a tolerable manner.

This book would not be complete without a few words about Joe Mountrose and his charming wife Kathleen. Doctor Joseph Mountrose has been my personal physician and valued friend for some thirty years, over the course of which we have maintained contact on virtually a daily basis. Not always for reasons connected with my health either.

Since I had the operation for cancer, Joe's extremely competent ministrations from his Harley Street premises, in hospitals, clinics and at home have been more valuable than I could ever express. I have been very fortunate to have him, not only as a loyal friend, but also as an eminent practioner.

We still enjoy very regular meals together. He and Kathleen are excellent company and it gives me much comfort and satisfaction to know that I am in such good hands. Although there is a long history of longevity in my family, there comes a time when everyone's life must draw to a close. Joe has, however, played a considerable part in ensuring that I am now well into my eighties and still going strong.

My duties as Founder President of Holiday Club Pontin's are not onerous by any means. The position provides me with an excuse to visit my former sites, not just as a visitor for nostalgic reasons – though these do play a part – but also to let everyone know that I am still around and keen to take an interest in what is going on.

Who knows, perhaps the children really are interested in catching sight of the man who started it all? I also attend various functions at the invitation of the board, such as the Red Cross holiday weeks, which give me great satisfaction.

My disappointments are now behind me. It is comforting to know that I can really enjoy these occasions without the need to count the light bulbs and complain about the size of the measures of whisky dispensed by the barmen – unless they are too small!

During site visits when I was really in top form my attention to detail was said to be legendary. I was determined that every member of the staff, from the manager downwards, was fully aware that a personal inspection by the Chairman and Managing Director could take place at any hour of the day or night.

I've mellowed now, of course, and 'The Guv'nor' is not around as much as he used to be.

Pontin's is as unique today as it was in 1970, when Southport, one of the new generation of holiday camps, was constructed and introduced to the market. The new owners have bought this site and others up to date.

I feel sure that they have applied their own talents to the expertise which has been accumulated since they first became involved with the company. The name has been retained and it seems clear that they have inherited my feeling for the business.

Holiday Club Pontin's now have twenty-two sites, compared to five with the Butlin's operation.

I once saw it written that 'A Pontin's holiday has become part of the British way of life'. This was in 1961, just 15 years after a war which cost a great number of lives and during which the British people made many sacrifices. I feel that the holiday camp industry made an important contribution to national recovery and I am proud to have played my part in the process.

I had the quotation in mind in the Spring of 1991 when I was told by a leading politician that I had been a 'National Asset'. It seems, then, that I have managed to leave my mark on Great Britain during a half-century of the family holiday industry.

I may no longer be a shareholder in Pontin's, but my heart is still very much with the business which still carries my family name.

Holiday Club Pontin's will continue to provide what their customers have come to appreciate over the years – value for money. Time can never stand still, but I very much hope and trust that the unique atmosphere which is Pontin's will continue for many seasons to come.

As for 'The Guv'nor', I can only hope that the doors will continue to open and prevent me from giving any thought to retirement. If such an idea should ever occur I shall lie on a couch in a darkened room until such time as the desire leaves me . . . and I can place my faith in the quotation from Milton's *Paradise Lost*: 'And short retirement urges sweet return'.

## SOURCE MATERIAL:

*The British Barker* – The Official Journal of the Variety Club of
   Great Britain

*The Millionaire Mentality* – by Michael Pearson
   Secker & Warburg

*The Pound in Your Pocket* – by Peter Wilsher
   Cassell & Company Limited

*Goodnight Campers – The History of the British Holiday Camp* –
   by Colin Ward and Dennis Hardy. Mansell

*Holiday Camps Directory and Magazine* – 1948 and 1949 editions

*Holiday Time at Butlin's* – 1951 edition

*Daily Telegraph* Library – newspaper cuttings

*New Encyclopaedia Britannica*, Volume 5, Micropaedia – ready
   reference edition

*Dictionary of National Biography* – Oxford University Press

*Dance News* and *Recall* – publications for ballroom dancers

Offer Document – Recommended Offer by Charterhouse Japhet
   Limited on behalf of Coral Leisure Group Limited for the whole
   of the share capital, issued and to be issued of Pontin's Limited

Records at the National Horseracing Museum, 99 High Street,
   Newmarket by kind permission of the Curator

*Who's Who 1990*

Extel Statistical Services Limited – Stock Exchange News Cards

BBC Television Light Entertainment Publicity – viewing figures

Pontin Family Tree – Mr L. Pontin

# INDEX